ADIL RASHID

ENGLAND CRICKETER

MR VIVEK KUMAR PANDEY

Contents

Foreword

Short Biography Of Adil Rashid & Life Style, Career etc. During Writing This Book No Character, No Religion & No Caste Are Harmed. It's Only For Study Purpose. We don't want to hurt anyone.

Preface

MY NAME IS VIVEK KUMAR PANDEY . I WAS BORN IN 30 SEP 2002,I AM FROM SURAT GUJARAT INDIA.MY DREAM WAS TO BE GOOD WRITERS ,MY FAMILY SUPPORTED ME TO SUCCESSFUL AND I CAN DO IT MY SELF.How do I write? That is a question, I believe, that can be honestly answered by me."CELEBRATING YOUNGEST WRITER AWARD WINNER IN GUJARAT 1ST RANK" MR PANDEY JI . I may think I did a good job writing something. The reader is the one who decides the quality of my writing. I do find writing to be natural to me and therefore find it to be a real challenge. My trick as a challenged writer is to do the best I can and know that I am happy with the final outcome. It may take a while to do my best and there may be quite a few problems I run into along the way.

I am not a greedy person those who are thinking about me and my self I never tried it anyone people suffering from sadness ,I trying to get promoted people suffering from happiness and joy in your Life Time. Now in current situation in India and also world people are unemployed and have no many but our indian governor help to people to get free food from ration card , i also take part in leadership team ,i am Motivational speaker , Film script writer. There was my two dream firstly writer and secondly actor & also my own film is upcoming soon i done almost completely completed script for my film .I AM GOING TO SAY WORD OF HEART TOUCH OUT PLEASE READ IT" , firstly i thanks my father he supports me in this field they always getting inspired me by own his words and behavior ,they always said that he was a biggest person in the world in future and also they purchase fruit and chocolate for me in anytime & anyway , firstly my father buy him then call me Vivek you want a chocolate i will say yes papa but how many tell me ,papa: you tell me how much i buy him i told 1 or 2 chocolate but my father purchase whole the boxes of chocolate and they get suprised me. MY FATHER WAS BORN IN " 20 SEPTEMBER" 1971 IN INDIA.

1) MY FATHER FAVORITE CLOTHES IS KURTA PAIJMA AND ALSO STYLES SHOE

2) FAVORITE SINGER IS KISHORE DA

3) FAVORITE STATE GUJARAT AND KOLKATA , HIS VILLAGE IN BIHAR

4) FAVORITE COLOR BLACK AND WHITE

THEY ALSO LOVE cricket like IPL and one day t-20 .they also like watching a News daily and heard the song daily ,they also interested in tik tok video but in current time tik tok is banned in india but also few videos are in you tube. In lockdown time my family and me very enjoy day daily. my father play daily ludo with his sister and son, daughter.they always loved tea and coffee anytime call me . I make it tea for my father but some reason after the April to june they are suffering from fever and cough , weakness on 6 June 2020 my father death. they not told me say bye bye his life. After death of 6 June on 10 june my mom and dad anniversary.but my father is Best in the world they can do anything for me please take care of father and respect it of your parents.

ONE
ADIL RASHID

- **Adil Rashid**

1. Short Biography Of Adil Rashid & Life Style, Career etc. During Writing This Book No Character, No Religion & No Caste Are Harmed. It's Only For Study Purpose. We don't want to hurt anyone.

Adil Rashid (born 17 February 1988) is an English cricketer who plays for England in One Day International (ODI) and Twenty20 International (T20I) cricket, and previously played for the Test team. In domestic cricket, he represents Yorkshire, and has played in multiple Twenty20 leagues, including for Punjab Kings in the Indian Premier League.

Rashid made his ODI and T20I debuts in 2009, and played for the Test team between 2015 and 2019. He was part of the England teams that won the 2019 Cricket World Cup and 2022 T20 World Cup.Rashid plays as a right-arm leg break bowler. He is England's highest wicket-taker among spin bowlers in both ODIs and T20Is, and England second-highest wicket-taker in T20Is overall behind Chris Jordan. Along with Jos Buttler, he holds the world record for highest seventh-wicket stand in ODIs: 177 against New Zealand in 2015.

Rashid was born in Bradford, West Yorkshire, and is of Pakistani background. Like his England teammate Moeen Ali, he belongs to the Mirpuri community, his family having migrated to England in 1967 from Mirpur, Jammu & Kashmir.His brothers Haroon and Amar are also cricketers.Rashid showed promise from a young age: Terry Jenner spotted him as a 14-year-old, and, in early July 2005, aged 17, he took 6–13 for Yorkshire's Academy (youth) team. A few days later he hit 111 for Yorkshire Cricket Board Under-17s against their Cheshire equivalents in the Under-17s County Championship.

In 2006, he played a number of games for Yorkshire Second XI, making four successive centuries. This form, combined with a calf injury to Darren Lehmann, earned him the chance to make his first-class debut.

• **Adil Rashid 2006: County debut and youth Tests**

Rashid made his county cricket debut against Warwickshire at North Marine Road, Scarborough, as a replacement for injured overseas batsman Darren Lehmann. In the second innings he bowled a magnificent 6/67 to rip through Warwickshire's middle order and win the match for Yorkshire. Rashid was then included in the England Under-19s Test squad for their series against India Under-19s. Making his debut for the side in the first Test at Canterbury, he scored 13 and 23 runs and took one wicket. In the second Test, at Taunton, he produced a dominant all-round display, scoring 114 and 48 and claiming 8/157 and 2/

45. He also played in the third Test at the Denis Compton Oval in Shenley, but made less of an impression, only taking three wickets and scoring 15 and 12 runs.

From mid-August until the end of the season, he held down a regular spot in the Yorkshire side. He continued to impress, taking 4/96 against Middlesex at Scarborough] and scoring 63, his maiden first-class half-century, against Nottinghamshire at Headingley as part of a fourth-wicket stand of 130 with Craig White to dig Yorkshire out of a hole from 42/3 before helping to bowl out Nottinghamshire's tail to win the match for Yorkshire. Rashid also featured in a two-day "spin match" held by the England and Wales Cricket Board, a programme which would simulate different match-based scenarios to develop young spin bowlers.

· Adil Rashid 2007: Young Player of the Year

During the winter, Rashid suffered from a stress fracture in his back and missed England Under-19s' tour of Malaysia, but he recovered well enough to be picked for the 2006–07 England A tour of Bangladesh. Despite unimpressive performances, he was tipped by Yorkshire teammate Jason Gillespie to play international cricket for England in the future.Adil is probably the best young cricketer in England. I think he could play an allround role for England in the future.

Rashid started the English summer at Lord's, playing for Marylebone Cricket Club (MCC) against the 2006 champion county, Sussex. In his County Championship game of the season, at The Oval against Surrey a few days later, he hit 86 in the first innings, putting on 190 with Jacques Rudolph for the sixth wicket. This established a new partnership record for the sixth wicket for Yorkshire against Surrey, surpassing a mark that had stood since 1902. At the end of April he continued to impress with bowling figures of 5/88 against Durham at Headingley. Due to his form he was picked to play for England Lions in a tour match against India.

Rashid was considered to play for England's Under-19 side again in their series against Pakistan, but his Yorkshire coach Martyn Moxon showed displeasure at the idea of Rashid being pulled away from county cricket. The selectors decided that as Rashid had progressed to the next level of cricket, having appeared for England Lions, and therefore he shouldn't be pulled out of county cricket to play for England Under-19s. In continuing to play county cricket, he scored his maiden first-class century, 108 against Worcestershire at Kidderminster, and another half-century against Warwickshire.

Over the course of the 2007 English cricket season, Rashid scored 837 with a batting average of 44.05 and took 43 wickets with a bowling average of 42.16 across all first-class matches. He took the most wickets of any Yorkshire player and scored the fourth-most runs. He won several awards in 2007 for his strong form. In June 2007 he won both the YCCSA Young Player of the Year Award for 2006 and the Neil Lloyd Young Cricketer of the Year Award for 2006. On 9 September Rashid was named 2007 Cricket Writers' Club Young Cricketer of the Year, while on 24 September he was awarded the title of PCA Young Player of the Year.In October 2007, Rashid was named in the "England Performance Programme squad", to train at home and in India during the 2007–08 winter.

· **Adil Rashid 2008: First tour with national team**

In January 2008, Rashid was named in the England Lions squad for the 2007–08 Duleep Trophy in India. He played two games for the tournament and took six wickets. For the second season in a row he was also named in the Marylebone Cricket Club squad to play against the champion county, this time Sussex. He also retained his place in the England Performance Programme squad.

There was concern early in the season that Rashid's bowling was losing some of its variety as it seemed his batting was taking precedence, but he then took career-best bowling figures of 7/107 against Hampshire at the Rose Bowl. He followed this up with hauls of 5/95 against Lancashire and 7/136 against Sussex. Rashid finished the season with 62 wickets, Yorkshire's leading wicket-taker for the second year in a row.

At the end of the year, Rashid was included in the English national team for their tour of India, though he wasn't expected to be any chance of playing a match for England, only being on the tour for the experience. He was then included in England's squad for their following tour of the West Indies, where he was part of England's team for a tour match against a Saint Kitts and Nevis team. National selector Geoff Miller, described Rashid's selection at the age of 20 in the following terms. Adil Rashid is an exciting prospect for the future and his inclusion will enable us to continue to monitor his development closely as well as providing extra competition for places in the spin-bowling department.

- **Adil Rashid 2009: World Twenty20 and ODI debut**

Rashid was again included in the England Lions team for a tour match against the West Indies, and he had a good all-round performance, scoring 72 runs in England Lions' first innings and taking 3/66 in the West Indies' second innings. Despite not being included in Yorkshire's side for their first two Twenty20 matches of the season, Rashid's form saw him called up to the national team for the 2009 ICC World Twenty20 as an injury replacement for Andrew Flintoff. In England's first warm-up match for the tournament against Scotland, Rashid appeared nervous, but in their second warm-up match against the West Indies he appeared more settled and took 1/20 from his 4 overs. During the tournament itself he had impressive performances against Pakistan and the West Indies, and he finished the tournament with 3 wickets at an average of 31.66 and with an economy of 7.30 runs per over from his 4 matches.

Following his World Twenty20 appearances, he was included in England's training squad for the 2009 Ashes series against Australia, thought to be a potential replacement for the out-of-form Monty Panesar, but instead of playing a warm-up game with the England XI he played with England Lions again in a tour match against Australia. He was left out of England's final squad for the Ashes and instead returned to playing county cricket with Yorkshire. Rashid scored his career-best 117 not out and later on helped Yorkshire to bowl Hampshire out with figures of 5/41. He then went on to better that against Lancashire, scoring an unbeaten 157 and taking 5/97 in the first innings. The feat of scoring a century and taking a five-for in a match was the third of his career; the last player to have achieved the feat twice in a season for Yorkshire was George Hirst back in 1911.

Rashid made his One Day International debut for England on 27 August 2009 against Ireland. He scored 7 runs and had bowling figures of 1/16 in a narrow win. He kept his place in the side for the 1st ODI against Australia, and he was the best of England's bowlers, only conceding 37 runs from his 10 overs. He followed this up with a quickfire 31 not out from just 23 balls with the bat to almost get England across the line in a tight finish. He impressed Australians Michael Clarke and James Hopes with his strong performance, but he was shockingly omitted from the English side for the next match. He did return for two more matches during the series, but finished with only 2 wickets at an average of 74.

· **Adil Rashid 2009–10: South Africa and Pakistan**

Rashid completely supplanted Monty Panesar in the England side, being named as the back-up to Graeme Swann for both the Test and ODI squads in their tour of South Africa. He played in the second Twenty20 International between the sides, but was only used for one over in which he conceded 25 runs, after which South Africa's coach Mickey Arthur criticized the English side for not showing enough faith in Rashid's ability. Due to an injury to Swann, Rashid was brought back into the side for the 2nd ODI, but he bowled an expensive three overs, conceding 27 runs, and was dropped once Swann was fit again.

He was then dropped from South Africa's ODI squad altogether for the rest of the series, instead playing four-day matches with the England Performance Programme. Meanwhile, offspinner James Tredwell remained on stand-by to potentially play, indicating that Rashid had dropped down the pecking order. His poor form continued in the England Performance Programme matches, and though he re-joined the main squad ahead of the Test series he did not play in any Test matches.

Following the poor tour for Rashid, he was left out of England's squad for their tour of Bangladesh, instead being sent to the United Arab Emirates to play for England Lions against Pakistan A. His time in the UAE was somewhat more successful than his time in South Africa, and he took 3/13 in the second Twenty20 against Pakistan A to secure a series win for England Lions. After the Twenty20 series against Pakistan A, England Lions also played a Twenty20 against the main England team and Rashid helped cause a shock upset win with another strong bowling performance of 3/22.

• Adil Rashid Continued domestic career

Following his unsuccessful winter abroad, Rashid returned to playing county cricket with Yorkshire in the 2010 summer. He immediately showed that he still had the potential to return to the English national team, showing his batting skills with an impressive innings against Warwickshire in his first match of the season. His self-confidence returned throughout the season and he had several impressive performances with both ball and bat in the county championship, finishing the season with 732 runs at 45.75 and 57 wickets at 31.29, as well as taking 26 wickets in the 2010 Twenty20 Cup, the most of the Yorkshire bowlers and the fourth-most overall. Despite his strong performances throughout the season he was still overlooked by English selectors, being left out of their home series against Bangladesh and the squad for the 2010–11 Ashes series in favour of Monty Panesar.

Not having been selected to play for England over the 2010–11 winter, Rashid instead played for South Australia in the 2010–11 KFC Twenty20 Big Bash. He played a useful role in the team alongside fellow spinner Nathan Lyon, and finished the season with 10 wickets, one behind the tournament's leaders Lyon and Pat Cummins, as South Australia won the tournament. Following the Big Bash, Rashid was selected to play for England Lions on a tour of the West Indies, during which they played in the local first-class competition, the 2010–11 Regional Four Day Competition.

· **Adil Rashid 2011–12: Decline in form**

Rashid started the 2011 season well by taking 6/77 and 5/37 in Yorkshire's opening match against Worcestershire, but overall he struggled for form, and conceded the worst bowling figures of his career, and the third-worst ever for Yorkshire, when he bowled no wicket for 187 runs against Sussex. His poor form continued into the 2012 season, and he found himself dropped from Yorkshire's team for the first time in his county career. This came as a result of his worst ever start to a county season, taking nine wickets at 49.00 in his first six matches. Yorkshire's president Geoffrey Boycott lamented that Rashid had not appeared to progress at all since he started playing county cricket, and said that Rashid needed to take responsibility for his poor performances. In ten first-class matches in 2012 he took just 16 wickets at an average of 41 and made 129 runs at 16.12, his decline meaning he was no longer even asked to play for England Lions anymore.

· **Adil Rashid 2013–14: Return to form**

Just hours before the start of the 2013 county season, Rashid was quoted by the Independent as saying that if his 2013 season didn't go well he'd request to go on loan from Yorkshire to a different county, which forced Yorkshire to deny that there was any rift between Rashid and the club. Martyn Moxon, then Yorkshire's director of cricket, said that the interview had been in January, months before the start of the season and that there hadn't been any issues. Rashid also showed that his poor form was behind him as he started the season with his highest first-class score, a 180 against Somerset. He followed this up with two more centuries, one against Warwickshire and a second against Somerset, taking his average for the county season up to that point above 200. In 2014 Rashid continued to improve his bowling, particularly in limited overs cricket, bowling career-best figures of 5/33 in a one-day match against Hampshire.In April 2022, he was bought by the Northern Superchargers for the 2022 season of The Hundred.

- **Adil Rashid 2014–15: South Africa A, West Indies and Ireland**

Due to his form in county cricket, Rashid was named in the England Lions squad for their tour of South Africa in early 2015, set to play in both their first-class and one-day series against South Africa A. He batted well on the tour with innings of 78 and 68 in the unofficial Tests. In March 2015, Rashid was named in the England Test squad for the tour of the West Indies. In the tour matches leading up to England's Test series against the West Indies, Rashid did not perform well enough to get into the Test side, with the selectors favouring James Tredwell ahead of him. Despite not being used in the Test matches, he was not allowed to return to England to play with Yorkshire at the beginning of the county cricket season, though Rashid did leave the tour early to join England's ODI team for their match against Ireland. After the match, Yorkshire hired a private jet to fly Rashid back in time for their next county match against Hampshire, where he took four wickets in each innings.

· **Rashid preparing to bowl again New Zealand in 2015**

With the 2015 Ashes around the corner, the English selectors decided to rest Moeen Ali from their ODI series against New Zealand and brought in Rashid as his replacement. Rashid had an immediate impact in the first match of the series, being involved in the highest 7th wicket partnership of ODI history with Jos Buttler, where they scored 177 runs. Rashid reached his maiden half-century in just 37 balls and went on to score 69 runs, then he gave the most eye-catching bowling of the match as well, making use of his googly to take the wicket of Kane Williamson and finishing with figures of 4/55. Rashid played all five matches of the series for England and finished with a total of 8 wickets.

Rashid was included in England's 13-man squad for the first Test of the Ashes, but the selectors decided that they would only use Rashid in the Test as a second spinner alongside Moeen Ali if there was a spinning pitch. Rashid remained in the Test squad for every match of the Ashes but did not play, and instead he continued playing county cricket for Yorkshire, scoring a century against Durham. Although he had not played in the Ashes at all, Rashid did get to play in the ODI series against Australia and solidified his spot in the team with figures of 4/59 in the 1st ODI and 2/41 in the 3rd ODI. Across the five-match series he took 7 wickets, the most of England's bowlers.

· Adil Rashid 2015 Pakistan

In October 2015, Rashid was selected in the England touring party to play Pakistan in the UAE making his debut in the First Test at Sheikh Zayed Cricket Stadium. Rashid had a torrid time in the first innings of his first match in the Test side, finishing with figures of 0-163 as Pakistan posted 523 - the worst figures by a Test debutant. However, he enjoyed a remarkable turn around of fortunes in the next innings, finishing with figures of 5-64, a return that was nearly good enough for England to win the match, although it eventually finished in a draw. In the second Test he took 1–84 in Pakistan's first innings and 1–107 in their second as England lost the game by 178 runs, although Rashid made his maiden Test half-century in England's second innings, hitting 61. In the third and final Test, Rashid did not take a wicket in Pakistan's first innings, and in the second innings he finished with 1-97 as England lost the match and the series 2–0.

Following the Test series, Rashid played in the ODI series. He only took one wicket in the first three games, finishing with figures of 0–60 in the first game, which England lost. After taking 1–32 in the second match, he again finished wicketless in the third match of the series. He was expensive in the final match of the series, although he did pick up three wickets and England won the match and the series 3–1.He played in all three of the T20 matches. After not bowling or batting in the first game, he took figures of 2–18 in the second game as England secured a three-run victory. He took 1–29 in the final game which went to a Super Over, with England winning the matches after the scores finished level.

· **Adil Rashid 2015/16 South Africa**

At the urging of coach Jason Gillespie, Rashid signed a deal to play for Adelaide Strikers in the Big Bash in 2015-16 after being left out of the England squad for the tour of South Africa.Rashid was not selected for the Test series against South Africa, although he did keep his place in the ODI side. After failing to take a wicket in the first game, he finished with figures of 1–43 in the second game which England won by five wickets. After taking 1–45 in the third game, he had his best return of the series in the fourth match. After making 39 with the bat, he took figures of 2-38, although South Africa secured a one wicket victory. In the final match of the series he took figures of 1-59 as South Africa won the match by five wickets to win the series 3–2. England lost both T20 matches, although Rashid performed reasonably well, taking figures of 1–24 in the first game and 1–30 in the second game, although England lost by nine wickets.

· **Adil Rashid 2016 T20 World Cup**

Rashid took figures of 1–20 in the opening game against the West Indies, although it wasn't enough to prevent a defeat. In the second game he picked up figures of 1–35 against South Africa, before taking his best figures of the tournament, 2–18 against Afghanistan. With England needing to beat Sri Lanka to qualify for the semi-finals, Rashid finished with figures of 0-31 as England won by ten runs. He did not pick up a wicket against New Zealand in the semi-final, but turned in a good performance in the final against West Indies, taking figures of 1-23. Despite his good performance, England suffered a narrow loss and finished as runners-up.

· Adil Rashid 2016 Sri Lanka and Pakistan

Rashid did not pick up a wicket in the first ODI, although he did bowl economically as the match ended in a tie. He took 2–34 in the second match of the series, which England won by ten wickets. In the rain affected third match, he failed to pick up a wicket, and the match was eventually abandoned. In the fourth ODI he took 2-47 as England won by six wickets. He picked up another two wickets in the final game of the series as England completed a 3–0 series win after winning the match by 122 runs. Rashid played in the only T20I between the two sides, and bowled economically, conceding just 25 runs from his four overs, as England won by eight wickets.

Rashid took figures of 2–51 in the first ODI against Pakistan, as England got off to a winning start. In the second ODI, he took figures of 1-51 as England restricted Pakistan to 251 and won the match by four wickets. In the third match of the series he took figures of 2-73 as England again won to go 3-0 up in the series. In the fourth match he took figures of 3-47 as England won by four wickets. Rashid was rested for the final match, which England lost. He took figures of 1–29 in the only T20I between the two sides, which England lost by nine wickets.

· Adil Rashid 2016 Bangladesh

In the first ODI against Bangladesh, Rashid took figures of 4–49 to help England to a 21-run victory. In the second match, he made an unbeaten 33 and took another two wickets, but England lost. In the third match of the series, he took 4-43 as England recorded a four wicket victory to win the series 2–1. In the first Test, Rashid scored 26 with the bat before taking 2-58. He took 1–55 in Bangladesh's second innings as England recorded a 22-run victory. In the second Test, Rashid was wicketless in the first innings but took 4–52 in the second innings. England were unable to chase down their target and lost by 108 runs.

· Adil Rashid 2016-17 India

In the first Test against India, Rashid took figures of 4–114 in India's first innings, before taking 3–64 in their second innings. However, England were unable to force a win and the match ended in a draw. Rashid took 2–110 in India's first innings of the second Test, before making an unbeaten 32 with the bat. He continued to bowl well in India's second innings, taking 4-82, although India won the game by 246 runs. In the third Test he took figures of 4–118 in India's first innings, before taking 1-28 as India secured an eight wicket victory. In the fourth Test, he took figures of 4–192 in India's first innings total of 631, as they won by an innings and 36 runs. In the final match of the series, he made 60 in England's first innings before taking figures of 1-153 as India posted 759/7 and won the match to win the series 4–0.

Rashid played in the first ODI against India and took figures of 0-50 as England lost by three wickets. He did not feature in the rest of the series, although he retained his place for the T20Is. In the first T20I he did not bat or bowl as England won by seven wickets. In the second match he took 1-24 but England lost by 5 runs as India levelled the series.

In the final match of the series he took figures of 0-23 as India made 202/6 and won by 75 runs.He was also named as part of the 'Team of the Tournament' at the 2017 Champions Trophy by the ICC, Cricinfo and Cricbuzz.

• Adil Rashid 2017 West Indies and Ireland

Rashid took 1–43 in the first ODI against the West Indies as England won by 45 runs. In the second match he took 2-53 as England secured a 4 wicket victory. Rashid made nine with bat as England made 328 in the final ODI, before taking 1–5 with the ball as England won by 186 runs to win the series 3–0. Later in the same year, the West Indies toured England. Rashid's first appearance was in the only T20I, in which he picked up a personal best of 3-25. He continued this good form into the ODI series, taking an economical 2–31 in the first of five, to help restrict the tourists to 204/9. England made light work of the total, as they cruised to a seven wicket victory. Despite the majority of the second ODI being abandoned due to rain, he took 3–34 in the third, while England won by 124 runs. In the final two games, Rashid picked up a solitary wicket in each, although England won both games and celebrated a 4–0 series victory as a consequence.

England started their summer by preparing for the Champions Trophy, which they were hosting for the second time in succession. Preparation began with two ODIs against Ireland. In the first ODI, Rashid picked up a career best of 5-27, as Ireland stumbled to 126 all out. England won the game comfortably; they cruised to a seven wicket victory. In the second ODI, Rashid made a speedy 39 from 25 deliveries, although his bowling proved to be less effective, as he took 1-68. England still managed to win the game by

85 runs, and take a 2–0 series victory.

· Adil Rashid 2018 Australia and India

Rashid played in all five ODIs against Australia, taking 12 wickets at an average of 21.50.In early 2018 Rashid informed Yorkshire of his desire to only play white-ball cricket during the upcoming season, and will not feature in the county championship for the side, preferring to focus on his limited-over career.Rashid was called up to the England squad to play Test cricket against India in the 2018 series, causing controversy after his decision not to play 4-day county cricket for Yorkshire. In the second Test, he became the first England cricketer for 13 years to complete a Test match without batting, bowling or taking a catch in the field.

· Adil Rashid 2019 West Indies and the Cricket World Cup

In England's tour of West Indies in 2019, Rashid was selected in all three squads. He played only one Test, in which his figures were 0–117. In the first ODI he took 3-74, with England winning by 6 wickets. In the second, he took 1–28 in a defeat. In the fourth ODI he took his second ODI five-for, with figures of 5–85 to help England to a 28-run victory.In April 2019, he was named in England's squad for the 2019 Cricket World Cup. On 21 June 2019, in the match against Sri Lanka, Rashid played in his 150th international match for England.

· Adil Rashid 2020 and 2021

On 29 May 2020, Rashid was named in a 55-man group of players to begin training ahead of international fixtures starting in England following the COVID-19 pandemic. On 9 July 2020, Rashid was included in England's 24-man squad to start training behind closed doors for the ODI series against Ireland. On 27 July 2020, Rashid was named in England's squad for the ODI series. In the second match against Ireland, he became the first spin bowler for England to take 150 wickets in ODIs. In November 2020, in the second fixture against South Africa, Rashid took his 50th wicket in T20I cricket.In September 2021, Rashid was named in England's squad for the 2021 ICC Men's T20 World Cup.

· **Adil Rashid Bowling style**

Rashid uses four different deliveries: the leg break, the top spinner, the googly and the slider.

TWO

ENGLAND CRICKET TEAM

- **England cricket team**

The England cricket team represents England and Wales in international cricket. Since 1997, it has been governed by the England and Wales Cricket Board (ECB), having been previously governed by Marylebone Cricket Club (the MCC) since 1903. England, as a founding nation, is a Full Member of the International Cricket Council (ICC) with Test, One Day International (ODI) and Twenty20 International (T20I) status. Until the 1990s, Scottish and Irish players also played for England as those countries were not yet ICC members in their own right.

England and Australia were the first teams to play a Test match (15–19 March 1877), and along with South Africa, these nations formed the Imperial Cricket Conference (the predecessor to today's International Cricket Council) on 15 June 1909. England and Australia also played the first ODI on 5 January 1971. England's first T20I was played on 13 June

2005, once more against Australia.

As of 20 December 2022, England have played 1,058 Test matches, winning 387 and losing 317 (with 354 draws). In Test series against Australia, England play for The Ashes, one of the most famous trophies in all of sport, and they have won the urn on 32 occasions. England have also played 773 ODIs, winning 389. They have appeared in the final of the Cricket World Cup four times, winning once in 2019; they have also finished as runners-up in two ICC Champions Trophies (2004 and 2013). England have played 170 T20Is, winning 90. They won the ICC T20 World Cup in 2010 and 2022, and were runners-up in 2016.As of 20 December 2022, England are ranked third in Tests, second in ODIs and second in T20Is by the ICC.

· **The All-England Eleven in 1846**

The first recorded incidence of a team with a claim to represent England comes from 9 July 1739 when an "All-England" team, which consisted of 11 gentlemen from any part of England exclusive of Kent, played against "the Unconquerable County" of Kent and lost by a margin of "very few notches". Such matches were repeated on numerous occasions for the best part of a century.In 1846 William Clarke formed the All-England Eleven. This team eventually competed against a United All-England Eleven with annual matches occurring between 1847 and 1856. These matches were arguably the most important contest of the English season if judged by the quality of the players.

· **The 1859 English team to North America.**

The first overseas tour occurred in September 1859 with England touring North America. This team had six players from the All-England Eleven, six from the United All-England Eleven and was captained by George Parr. With the outbreak of the American Civil War, attention turned elsewhere. English tourists visited Australia in 1861–62 with this first tour organised as a commercial venture by Messrs Spiers and Pond, restaurateurs of Melbourne. Most matches played during tours prior to 1877 were "against odds", with the opposing team fielding more than 11 players to make for a more even contest. This first Australian tour were mostly against odds of at least 18/11.

- **The first England team to tour southern Australia in 1861–62**

The tour was so successful that Parr led a second tour in 1863–64. James Lillywhite led a subsequent England team which sailed on the P&O steamship Poonah on 21 September 1876. They played a combined Australian XI, for once on even terms of 11-a-side. The match, starting on 15 March 1877 at the Melbourne Cricket Ground came to be regarded as the inaugural Test match. The combined Australian XI won this Test match by 45 runs with Charles Bannerman of Australia scoring the first Test century. At the time, the match was promoted as James Lillywhite's XI v Combined Victoria and New South Wales. The teams played a return match on the same ground at Easter, 1877, when Lillywhite's team avenged their loss with a victory by four wickets. The first Test match on English soil occurred in 1880 with England victorious; this was the first time England fielded a fully representative side with W. G. Grace included in the team.

· **1880s**

As a result of this loss, the tour of 1882–83 was dubbed by England captain Ivo Bligh as "the quest to regain the ashes". England, with a mixture of amateurs and professionals, won the series 2–1. Bligh was presented with an urn that contained some ashes, which have variously been said to be of a bail, ball or even a woman's veil, and so The Ashes was born. A fourth match was then played which Australia won by four wickets. However, the match was not considered part of the Ashes series. England dominated many of these early contests, with England winning the Ashes series 10 times between 1884 and 1898. During this period England also played their first Test match against South Africa in 1889 at Port Elizabeth.

· **1890s**

England won the 1890 Ashes series 2–0, with the third match of the series being the first Test match to be abandoned. England lost 2–1 in the 1891–92 series, although England regained the urn the following year. England again won the 1894–95 series, winning 3–2 under the leadership of Andrew Stoddart. In 1895–96, England played South Africa, winning all Tests in the series. The 1899 Ashes series was the first tour where the MCC and the counties appointed a selection committee. There were three active players: Grace, Lord Hawke and Warwickshire captain Herbert Bainbridge. Prior to this, England teams for home Tests had been chosen by the club on whose ground the match was to be played. England lost the 1899 Ashes series 1–0, with Grace making his final Test appearance in the first match of the series.

- **1900s**

The start of the 20th century saw mixed results for England as they lost four of the eight Ashes series between 1900 and 1914. During this period, England lost their first series against South Africa in the 1905–06 season 4–1 as their batting faltered.England lost their first series of the new century to Australia in 1901–02 Ashes. Australia also won the 1902 series, which was memorable for exciting cricket, including Gilbert Jessop scoring a Test century in just 70 minutes. England regained the Ashes in 1904 under the captaincy of Pelham Warner. R. E. Foster scored 287 on his debut and Wilfred Rhodes took 15 wickets in a match. In 1905–06, England lost 4–1 against South Africa. England avenged the defeat in 1907, when they won the series 1–0 under the captaincy of Foster. However, they lost the 1909 Ashes series against Australia, suing 25 players in the process. England also lost to South Africa, with Jack Hobbs scoring his first of 15 centuries on the tour.

- **1910s**

England toured Australia in 1911–12 and beat their opponents 4–1. The team included the likes of Rhodes, Hobbs, Frank Woolley and Sydney Barnes. England lost the first match of the series but bounced back and won the next four Tests. This proved to be the last Ashes series before the war.The 1912 season saw England take part in a unique experiment. A nine-Test triangular tournament involving England, South Africa and Australia was set up. The series was hampered by a very wet summer and player disputes however and the tournament was considered a failure with the Daily Telegraph stating.Nine Tests provide a surfeit of cricket, and contests between Australia and South Africa are not a great attraction to the British public.

With Australia sending a weakened team and the South African bowlers being ineffective England dominated the tournament winning four of their six matches. The match between Australia and South Africa at Lord's was visited by King George V, the first time a reigning monarch had watched Test cricket. England went on one more tour before the outbreak of the First World War, beating South Africa 4–0, with Barnes taking 49 wickets in the series.

· **1920s**

English cricket team at the Test match at the Brisbane Exhibition Ground in 1928. England won by a record margin of 675 runs.England's first match after the war was in the 1920–21 season against Australia. Still feeling the effects of the war England went down to a series of crushing defeats and suffered their first whitewash losing the series 5–0. Six Australians scored hundreds while Mailey spun out 36 English batsmen. Things were no better in the next few Ashes series losing the 1921 Ashes series 3–0 and the 1924–25 Ashes 4–1. England's fortunes were to change in 1926 as they regained the Ashes and were a formidable team during this period dispatching Australia 4–1 in the 1928–29 Ashes tour.

On the same year the West Indies became the fourth nation to be granted Test status and played their first game against England. England won each of these three Tests by an innings, and a view was expressed in the press that their elevation had proved a mistake although Learie Constantine did the double on the tour. In the 1929–30 season England went on two concurrent tours with one team going to New Zealand (who were granted Test status earlier that year) and the other to the West Indies. Despite sending two separate teams England won both tours beating New Zealand 1–0 and the West Indies 2–1.

· **1930s**

Bill Woodfull evades a Bodyline ball. Note the number of leg-side fielders.The 1930 Ashes series saw a young Don Bradman dominate the tour, scoring 974 runs in his seven Test innings. He scored 254 at Lord's, 334 at Headingley and 232 at The Oval. Australia regained the Ashes winning the series 3–1. As a result of Bradman's prolific run-scoring the England captain Douglas Jardine chose to develop the already existing leg theory into fast leg theory, or bodyline, as a tactic to stop Bradman. Fast leg theory involved bowling fast balls directly at the batsman's body. The batsman would need to defend himself, and if he touched the ball with the bat, he risked being caught by one of a large number of fielders placed on the leg side.

Using Jardine's fast leg theory, England won the next Ashes series 4–1, but complaints about the Bodyline tactic caused crowd disruption on the tour, and threats of diplomatic action from the Australian Cricket Board, which during the tour sent the following cable to the MCC in London:

Bodyline bowling assumed such proportions as to menace best interests of game, making protection of body by batsmen the main consideration. Causing intensely bitter feeling between players as well as injury. In our opinion is unsportsmanlike. Unless stopped at once likely to upset friendly relations existing between Australia and England.Later, Jardine was removed from the captaincy and the Laws of Cricket changed so that no more than one fast ball aimed at the body was permitted per over, and having more than two fielders behind square leg was banned.

England's following tour of India in the 1933–34 season was the first Test match to be staged in the subcontinent. The series was also notable for Stan Nichols and Nobby Clark bowling so many bouncers that the Indian batsman wore solar toupées instead of caps to protect themselves.Australia won the 1934 Ashes series 2–1 and kept the urn for the following 19 years. Many of the wickets of the time were friendly to batsmen resulting in a large proportion of matches ending in high scoring draws and many batting records being set.

England drew the 1938 Ashes, meaning Australia retained the urn. England went into the final match of the series at The Oval 1–0 down, but won the final game by an innings and 579 runs. Len Hutton made the highest ever Test score by an Englishman, making 364 in England first innings to help them reach 903, their highest ever score against Australia.

The 1938–39 tour of South Africa saw another experiment with the deciding Test being a timeless Test that was played to a finish. England lead 1–0 going into the final timeless match at Durban. Despite the final Test being 'timeless', the game ended in a draw after 10 days as England had to catch the train to catch the boat home. A record 1,981 runs were scored, and the concept of timeless Tests was abandoned. England went on one final tour of the West Indies in 1939 before the Second World War, although a team for an MCC tour of India was selected more in hope than expectation of the matches being played.

· **1940s**

Test cricket resumed after the war in 1946, and England won their first match back against India. However, they struggled in the 1946–47 Ashes series, losing 3–0 in Australia under Wally Hammond's captaincy. England beat South Africa 3–0 in 1947 with Denis Compton scoring 1,187 runs in the series.

The 1947–48 series against the West Indies was another disappointment for England, with the side losing 2–0 following injuries to several key players. England suffered further humiliation against Bradman's invincible side in the 1948 Ashes series. Hutton was controversially dropped for the third Test, and England were bowled out for just 52 at The Oval. The series proved to be Bradman's final Ashes series.

In 1948–49, England beat South Africa 2–0 under the captaincy of George Mann. The series included a record breaking stand of 359 between Hutton and Cyril Washbrook. The decade ended with England drawing the Test series against New Zealand, with every match ending in a draw.

· **1950s**

Their fortunes changed on the 1953 Ashes tour as they won the series 1–0. England did not lose a series between their 1950–51 and 1958–59 tours of Australia and secured famous victory in 1954–55 under the captaincy of Len Hutton, thanks to Frank Tyson whose 6/85 at Sydney and 7/27 at Melbourne are remembered as the fastest bowling ever seen in Australia. The 1956 series was remembered for the bowling of Jim Laker who took 46 wickets at an average of 9.62, including figures of 19/90 at Old Trafford. After drawing to South Africa, England defeated the West Indies and New Zealand comfortably.

The England team then left for Australia in the 1958–59 season with a team that had been hailed as the strongest ever to leave on an Ashes tour but lost the series 4–0 as Richie Benaud's revitalised Australians were too strong, with England struggling with the bat throughout the series.On 24 August 1959, England inflicted its only 5–0 whitewash over India. All out for 194 at The Oval, India lost the last test by an innings. England's batsman Ken Barrington and Colin Cowdrey both had an excellent series with the bat, with Barrington scoring 357 runs across the series and Cowdrey scoring 344.

· **1960s**

The early and middle 1960s were poor periods for English cricket. Despite England's strength on paper, Australia held the Ashes and the West Indies dominated England in the early part of the decade. May stood down as captain in 1961 following the 1961 Ashes defeat.

Ted Dexter succeeded him as captain but England continued to suffer indifferent results. In 1961–62, they beat Pakistan, but also lost to India. The following year saw England and Australia tie the 1962–63 Ashes series 1–1, meaning Australia retained the urn. Despite beating New Zealand 3–0, England went on to lose to the West Indies, and again failed in the 1964 Ashes, losing the home series 1–0, which marked the end of Dexter's captaincy.

However, from 1968 to 1971 they played 27 consecutive Test matches without defeat, winning 9 and drawing 18 (including the abandoned Test at Melbourne in 1970–71). The sequence began when they drew with Australia at Lord's in the Second Test of the 1968 Ashes series and ended in 1971 when India won the Third Test at The Oval by four wickets. They played 13 Tests with only one defeat immediately beforehand and so played a total of 40 consecutive Tests with only one defeat, dating from their innings victory over the West Indies at The Oval in 1966. During this period they beat New Zealand, India, the West Indies, and Pakistan, and under Ray Illingworth's leadership, regained The Ashes from Australia in 1970–71.

· 1970s

The 1970s, for the England team, can be largely split into three parts. Early in the decade, Illingworth's side dominated world cricket, winning the Ashes away in 1971 and then retaining them at home in 1972. The same side beat Pakistan at home in 1971 and played by far the better cricket against India that season. However, England were largely helped by the rain to sneak the Pakistan series 1–0 but the same rain saved India twice and one England collapse saw them lose to India. This was, however, one of (if not the) strongest England team ever with the likes of Illingworth, Geoffrey Boycott, John Edrich, Basil D'Oliveira, Dennis Amiss, Alan Knott, John Snow and Derek Underwood at its core.

The mid-1970s were more turbulent. Illingworth and several others had refused to tour India in 1972–73 which led to a clamour for Illingworth's job by the end of that summer – England had just been beaten 2–0 by a flamboyant West Indies side – with several England players well over 35. Mike Denness was the surprising choice but only lasted 18 months; his results against poor opposition were good, but England were badly exposed as ageing and lacking in good fast bowling against the 1974–75

Australians, losing that series 4–1 to lose the Ashes.Denness was replaced in 1975 by Tony Greig. While he managed to avoid losing to Australia, his side were largely thrashed the following year by the young and very much upcoming West Indies for whom Greig's infamous "grovel" remark acted as motivation. Greig's finest hour was probably the 1976–77 win over India in India. When Greig was discovered as being instrumental in World Series Cricket, he was sacked, and replaced by Mike Brearley.

Brearley's side showed again the hyperbole that is often spoken when one side dominates in cricket. While his side of 1977–80 contained some young players who went on to become England greats, most notably future captains Ian Botham, David Gower and Graham Gooch, their opponents were often very much weakened by the absence of their World Series players, especially in 1978, when England beat New Zealand 3–0 and Pakistan 2–0 before thrashing what was effectively Australia's 2nd XI 5–1 in 1978–79.

· 1980s

The England team, with Brearley's exit in 1980, was never truly settled throughout the 1980s, which will probably be remembered as a low point for the team. While some of the great players like Botham, Gooch and Gower had fine careers, the team seldom succeeded in beating good opposition throughout the decade and did not score a home Test victory (except against minnows Sri Lanka) between September 1985 and July 1990.

Botham took over the captaincy in 1980 and they put up a good fight against the West Indies, losing a five match Test series 1–0, although England were humbled in the return series. After scoring a pair in the first Test against Australia,

Botham lost the captaincy due to his poor form, and was replaced by Brearley. Botham returned to form and played exceptionally in the remainder of the series, being named man of the match in the third, fourth and fifth Tests. The series became known as Botham's Ashes as England recorded a 3–1 victory.

Keith Fletcher took over as captain in 1981, but England lost his first series in charge against India. Bob Willis took over as captain in 1982 and enjoyed victories over India and Pakistan, but lost the Ashes after Australia clinched the series 2–1. England hosted the World Cup in 1983 and reached the semi-finals, but their Test form remained poor, as they suffered defeats against New Zealand, Pakistan and the West Indies.Gower took over as skipper in 1984 and led the team to a 2–1 victory over India. They went on to win the 1985 Ashes 3–1, although after this came a poor run of form. Defeat to the West Indies dented the team's confidence, and they went on to lose to India 2–0. In 1986, Micky Stewart was appointed the first full-time England coach. England beat New Zealand, but there was little hope of them retaining the Ashes in 1986–87. However, despite being described as a team that 'can't bat, can't bowl and can't field', they went on to win the series 2–1.

After losing consecutive series against Pakistan, England drew a three match Test series against New Zealand 0–0. They reached the final of the 1987 World Cup, but lost by seven runs against Australia. After losing 4–0 to the West Indies, England lost the Ashes to a resurgent Australia led by Allan Border. With the likes of Gooch banned following a rebel tour to South Africa, a new look England side suffered defeat again against the West Indies, although this time by a margin of 2–1.

· **1990s**

If the 1980s were a low point for English Test cricket, then the 1990s were only a slight improvement. The arrival of Gooch as captain in 1990 forced a move toward more professionalism and especially fitness though it took some time for old habits to die. Even in 2011, one or two successful county players have been shown up as physically unfit for international cricket. Creditable performances against India and New Zealand in 1990 were followed by a hard-fought draw against the 1991 West Indies and a strong performance in the 1992 Cricket World Cup in which the England team finished as runners-up for the second consecutive World Cup, but landmark losses against Australia in 1990–91 and especially Pakistan in 1992 showed England up badly in terms of bowling. So bad was England's bowling in 1993 that Rod Marsh described England's pace attack at one point as "pie throwers". Having lost three of the first four Tests played in England in 1993, Gooch resigned to be replaced by Michael Atherton.

More selectorial problems abounded during Atherton's reign as new chairman of selectors and coach Ray Illingworth (then into his 60s) assumed almost sole responsibility for the team off the field. The youth policy which had seen England emerge from the West Indies tour of 1993–94 with some credit (though losing to a seasoned Windies team) was abandoned and players such as Gatting and Gooch were persisted with when well into their 30s and 40s. England continued to do well at home against weaker opponents such as India, New Zealand and a West Indies side beginning to fade but struggled badly against improving sides like Pakistan and South Africa. Atherton had offered his resignation after losing the 1997 Ashes series 3–2 having been 1–0 up after two matches – eventually to resign one series later in early 1998. England, looking for talent, went through a whole raft of new players during this period, such as Ronnie Irani, Adam Hollioake, Craig White, Graeme Hick and Mark Ramprakash. At this time, there were two main problems:

The lack of a genuine all-rounder to bat at 6, Botham having left a huge gap in the batting order when he retired from Tests in 1992.Alec Stewart, a sound wicket-keeper and an excellent player of quick bowling, could not open and keep wicket, hence his batting down the order, where he was often exposed to spin which he did not play as well.

Stewart took the reins as captain in 1998, but another losing Ashes series and early World Cup exit cost him Test and ODI captaincy in 1999. This should not detract from the 1998 home Test series where England showed great fortitude to beat a powerful South African side 2–1.

Another reason for their poor performances were the demands of County Cricket teams on their players, meaning that England could rarely field a full-strength team on their tours. This eventually led to the ECB taking over from the MCC as the governing body of England and the implementation of central contracts. 1992 also saw Scotland sever ties with the England and Wales team, and begin to compete as the Scotland national team.

By 1999, with coach David Lloyd resigning after the World Cup exit and new captain Nasser Hussain just appointed, England hit rock bottom (literally ranked as the lowest-rated Test nation) after losing 2–1 to New Zealand in shambolic fashion. Hussain was booed on the Oval balcony as the crowd jeered "We've got the worst team in the world" to the tune of "He's Got the Whole World in His Hands".

· **2000s**

Central contracts were installed – reducing players workloads – and following the arrival of Zimbabwean coach Duncan Fletcher, England thrashed the fallen West Indies 3–1. England's results in Asia improved that winter with series wins against both Pakistan and Sri Lanka. Hussain's side had a far harder edge to it, avoiding the anticipated "Greenwash" in the 2001 Ashes series against the all-powerful Australian team. The nucleus the side was slowly coming together as players such as Hussain himself, Graham Thorpe, Darren Gough and Ashley Giles began to be regularly selected. By 2003 though, having endured another Ashes drubbing as well as another first-round exit from the World Cup, Hussain resigned as captain after one Test against South Africa.

Michael Vaughan took over, with players encouraged to express themselves. England won five consecutive Test series prior to facing Australia in the 2005 Ashes series, taking the team to second place in the ICC Test Championship table. During this period England defeated the West Indies home and away, New Zealand, and Bangladesh at home, and South Africa in South Africa. In June 2005, England played its first ever T20 international match, defeating Australia by 100 runs. Later that year, England defeated Australia 2–1 in a thrilling series to regain the Ashes for the first time in 16 years, having lost them in 1989. Following the 2005 Ashes win, the team suffered from a spate of serious injuries to key players such as Vaughan, Giles, Andrew Flintoff and Simon Jones. As a result, the team underwent an enforced period of transition. A 2–0 defeat in Pakistan was followed by two drawn away series with India and Sri Lanka.

In the home Test series victory against Pakistan in July and August 2006, several promising new players emerged. Most notable were the left-arm orthodox spin bowler Monty Panesar, the first Sikh to play Test cricket for England, and left-handed opening batsman Alastair Cook. The 2006–07 Ashes series was keenly anticipated and was expected to provide a level of competition comparable to the 2005 series. In the event, England, captained by Flintoff who was deputising for the injured Vaughan, lost all five Tests to concede the first Ashes whitewash in 86 years.

In the 2007 Cricket World Cup, England lost to most of the Test playing nations they faced, beating only the West Indies and Bangladesh, although they also avoided defeat by any of the non-Test playing nations. Even so, the unimpressive nature of most of their victories in the tournament, combined with heavy defeats by New Zealand, Australia and South Africa, left many commentators criticising the manner in which the England team approached the one-day game. Coach Duncan Fletcher resigned after eight years in the job as a result and was succeeded by former Sussex coach Peter Moores.

In 2007–08, England toured Sri Lanka and New Zealand, losing the first series 1–0 and winning the second 2–1. These series were followed up at home in May 2008 with a 2–0 home series win against New Zealand, with the results easing pressure on Moores – who was not at ease with his team, particularly star batsman Kevin Pietersen. Pietersen succeeded Vaughan as captain in June 2008, after England had been well beaten by South Africa at home. The poor relationship between the two came to a head on the 2008–09 tour to India. England lost the series 1–0 and both men resigned their positions, although Pietersen remained a member of the England team. Moores was replaced as coach by Zimbabwean Andy Flower. Against this background, England toured the West Indies under the captaincy of Andrew Strauss and, in a disappointing performance, lost the Test series 1–0.

The 2009 Ashes series featured the first Test match played in Wales, at Sophia Gardens, Cardiff. England drew the match thanks to a last-wicket stand by bowlers James Anderson and Panesar. A victory for each team followed before the series was decided at The Oval. Thanks to fine bowling by Stuart Broad and Graeme Swann and a debut century by Jonathan Trott, England regained the Ashes.

· **2010s**

2019 World cup winning team with prime minister Theresa May After a drawn Test series in South Africa, England won their first ever ICC world championship, the 2010 World Twenty20, with a seven-wicket win over Australia in Barbados. The following winter in the 2010–11 Ashes, they beat Australia 3–1 to retain the urn and record their first series win in Australia for 24 years. Furthermore, all three of their wins were by an innings – the first time a touring side had ever recorded three innings victories in a single Test series. Cook earned Man of the Series with 766 runs.

England struggled to match their Test form in the 2011 Cricket World Cup. Despite beating South Africa and tying with eventual winners India, England suffered shock losses to Ireland and Bangladesh before losing in the quarter-finals to Sri Lanka. However the team's excellent form in the Test match arena continued and on 13 August 2011, they became the world's top-ranked Test team after comfortably whitewashing India 4–0, their sixth consecutive series victory and eighth in the past nine series. However, this status only lasted a year – having lost 3–0 to Pakistan over the winter, England were beaten 2–0 by South Africa, who replaced them at the top of the rankings. It was their first home series loss since 2008, against the same opposition.

This loss saw the resignation of Strauss as captain (and his retirement from cricket). Cook, who was already in charge of the ODI side, replaced Strauss and led England to a 2–1 victory in India – their first in the country since 1984–85. In doing so, he became the first captain to score centuries in his first five Tests as captain and became England's leading century-maker with 23 centuries to his name.

- **The England team celebrate victory over Australia in the 2015 Ashes series**

After finishing as runners-up in the ICC Champions Trophy, England faced Australia in back-to-back Ashes series. A 3–0 home win secured England the urn for the fourth time in five series. However, in the return series, they found themselves utterly demolished in a 5–0 defeat, their second Ashes whitewash in under a decade. Their misery was compounded by batsman Jonathan Trott leaving the tour early due to a stress-related illness and the mid-series retirement of spinner Graeme Swann. Following the tour, head coach Flower resigned his post while Pietersen was dropped indefinitely from the England team. Flower was replaced by his predecessor, Moores, but he was sacked for a second time after a string of disappointing results including failing to advance from the group stage at the 2015 World Cup. He was replaced by Australian Trevor Bayliss who oversaw an upturn of form in the ODI side, including series victories against New Zealand and Pakistan. In the Test arena, England reclaimed the Ashes 3–2 in the summer of 2015.

England entered the 2019 Cricket World Cup as favourites, having been ranked the number one ODI side by the ICC for over a year prior to the tournament. However, shock defeats to Pakistan and Sri Lanka during the group stage left them on the brink of elimination and needing to win their final two games against India and New Zealand to guarantee progression to the semi-finals. This was achieved, putting their campaign back on track, and an eight-wicket victory over Australia in the semi-final at Edgbaston meant England were in their first World Cup final since 1992. The final against New Zealand at Lord's has been described as one of the greatest and most dramatic matches in the history of cricket, with some calling it the "greatest ODI in history", as both the match and subsequent Super Over were tied, after England went into the final over of their innings 14 runs behind New Zealand's total. England won by virtue of having scored more boundaries throughout the match, securing their maiden World Cup title in their fourth final appearance.

· England and Wales Cricket Board

The England and Wales Cricket Board (ECB) is the governing body of English cricket and the England cricket team. The Board has been operating since 1 January 1997 and represents England on the International Cricket Council. The ECB is also responsible for the generation of income from the sale of tickets, sponsorship and broadcasting rights, primarily in relation to the England team. The ECB's income in the 2006 calendar year was £77 million.

Prior to 1997, the Test and County Cricket Board (TCCB) was the governing body for the English team. Apart from in Test matches, when touring abroad, the England team officially played as MCC up to and including the 1976–77 tour of Australia, reflecting the time when MCC had been responsible for selecting the touring party. The last time the England touring team wore the bacon-and-egg colours of the MCC was on the 1996–97 tour of New Zealand.

- **Status of Wales**

Historically, the England team represented the whole of Great Britain in international cricket, with Scottish or Welsh national teams playing sporadically and players from both countries occasionally representing England. Scotland became an independent member of the ICC in 1994, having severed links with the TCCB two years earlier.

Criticism has been made of the England and Wales Cricket Board using only the England name while utilising Welsh players such as Simon and Geraint Jones. With Welsh players pursuing international careers exclusively with an England team, there have been a number of calls for Wales to become an independent member of the ICC, or for the ECB to provide more fixtures for a Welsh national team. However, both Cricket Wales and Glamorgan County Cricket Club have continually supported the ECB, with Glamorgan arguing for the financial benefits of the Welsh county within the English structure, and Cricket Wales stating they are "committed to continuing to play a major role within the ECB"

The absence of a Welsh cricket team has seen a number of debates within the Welsh Senedd. In 2013 a debate saw both Conservative and Labour members lend their support to the establishment of an independent Welsh team.

In 2015, a report produced by the Welsh National Assembly's petitions committee, reflected the passionate debate around the issue. Bethan Jenkins, Plaid Cymru's spokesperson on heritage, culture, sport and broadcasting, and a member of the petitions committee, argued that Wales should have its own international team and withdraw from the ECB. Jenkins noted that Ireland (with a population of 6.4 million) was an ICC member with 6,000 club players whereas Wales (with 3 million) had 7,500. Jenkins said: "Cricket Wales and Glamorgan CCC say the idea of a Welsh national cricket team is 'an emotive subject', of course having a national team is emotive, you only have to look at the stands during any national game to see that. To suggest this as anything other than natural is a bit of a misleading argument."

In 2017, the First Minister of Wales, Carwyn Jones called for the reintroduction of the Welsh one-day team stating: " is odd that we see Ireland and Scotland playing in international tournaments and not Wales."

· **Team colours**

1. 1994–1996Tetley Bitter
2. 1996–1998ASICS
3. 1998–2000Vodafone
4. 2000–2008Admiral
5. 2008–2010Adidas
6. 2010–2014Brit Insurance
7. 2014–2017Waitrose
8. 2017–2021New BalanceNatWest
9. 2021–2022Cinch

10. 2022–presentCastore

In February 2021, England and Wales Cricket Board announced that England's Principal partner NatWest has been replaced by Cinch, an online used car marketplace. England's kit is manufactured by Castore, who replaced previous manufacturer New Balance in April 2022.

When playing Test cricket, England's cricket whites feature the three lions badge on the left of the shirt and the name of the sponsor Cinch on the centre. English fielders may wear a navy blue cap or white sun hat with the ECB logo in the middle. Helmets are also coloured navy blue. Before 1997 the uniform sported the TCCB lion and stumps logo on the uniforms, while the helmets, jumpers and hats had the three lions emblem.

In limited overs cricket, England's ODI and Twenty20 shirts feature the Cinch logo across the centre, with the three lions badge on the left of the shirt and the New Balance logo on the right. In ODIs, the kit comprises a blue shirt with navy trousers, whilst the Twenty20 kit comprises a flame red shirt and navy trousers. In ICC limited-overs tournaments, a modified kit design is used with sponsor's logo moving to the sleeve and 'ENGLAND' printed across the front.Over the years, England's ODI kit has cycled between various shades of blue (such as a pale blue used until the mid-1990s, when it was replaced in favour of a bright blue)with the occasional all-red kit.In April 2017, ECB brought back traditional cable-knit sweater for test matches under new supplier New Balance.

THREE

LET'S KNOW ABOUT CRICKET

- **Let's Know About Cricket**

Cricket is a bat-and-ball game played between two teams of eleven players on a field at the centre of which is a 22-yard (20-metre) pitch with a wicket at each end, each comprising two bails balanced on three stumps. The game proceeds when a player on the fielding team, called the bowler, "bowls" (propels) the ball from one end of the pitch towards the wicket at the other end. The batting side's players score runs by striking the bowled ball with a bat and running between the wickets, while the bowling side tries to prevent this by keeping the ball within the field and getting it to either wicket, and dismiss each batter (so they are "out"). Means of dismissal include being bowled, when the ball hits the stumps and dislodges the bails, and by the fielding side either catching a hit ball before it touches the ground, or hitting a wicket with the ball before a batter can cross the crease line in front of the wicket to complete a run. When ten batters have been dismissed, the innings ends and the teams swap roles. The game is adjudicated by two umpires, aided by a third umpire and match referee in international matches.

Forms of cricket range from Twenty20, with each team batting for a single innings of 20 overs and the game generally lasting three hours, to Test matches played over five days. Traditionally cricketers play in all-white kit, but in limited overs cricket they wear club or team colours. In addition to the basic kit, some players wear protective gear to prevent injury caused by the ball, which is a hard, solid spheroid made of compressed leather with a slightly raised sewn seam enclosing a cork core layered with tightly wound string.

The earliest reference to cricket is in South East England in the mid-16th century. It spread globally with the expansion of the British Empire, with the first international matches in the second half of the 19th century. The game's governing body is the International Cricket Council (ICC), which has over 100 members, twelve of which are full members who play Test matches. The game's rules, the Laws of Cricket, are maintained by Marylebone Cricket Club (MCC) in London. The sport is followed primarily in South Asia, Australasia, the United Kingdom, southern Africa and the West Indies.Women's cricket, which is organised and played separately, has also achieved international standard. The most successful side playing international cricket is Australia, which has won seven One Day International trophies, including five World Cups, more than any other country and has been the top-rated Test side more than any other country.

- **History of cricket to 1725**

Cricket is one of many games in the "club ball" sphere that basically involve hitting a ball with a hand-held implement; others include baseball (which shares many similarities with cricket, both belonging in the more specific bat-and-ball games category), golf, hockey, tennis, squash, badminton and table tennis. In cricket's case, a key difference is the existence of a solid target structure, the wicket (originally, it is thought, a "wicket gate" through which sheep were herded), that the batter must defend. The cricket historian Harry Altham identified three "groups" of "club ball" games: the "hockey group", in which the ball is driven to and fro between two targets (the goals); the "golf group", in which the ball is driven towards an undefended target (the hole); and the "cricket group", in which "the ball is aimed at a mark (the wicket) and driven away from it".

It is generally believed that cricket originated as a children's game in the south-eastern counties of England, sometime during the medieval period.Although there are claims for prior dates, the earliest definite reference to cricket being played comes from evidence given at a court case in Guildford in January 1597 (Old Style), equating to January 1598 in the modern calendar. The case concerned ownership of a certain plot of land and the court heard the testimony of a 59-year-old coroner, John Derrick, who gave witness that.

Being a scholler in the ffree schoole of Guldeford hee and diverse of his fellows did runne and play there at creckett and other plaies.

Given Derrick's age, it was about half a century earlier when he was at school and so it is certain that cricket was being played c. 1550 by boys in Surrey. The view that it was originally a children's game is reinforced by Randle Cotgrave's 1611 English-French dictionary in which he defined the noun "crosse" as "the crooked staff wherewith boys play at cricket" and the verb form "crosser" as "to play at cricket".

One possible source for the sport's name is the Old English word "cryce" (or "cricc") meaning a crutch or staff. In Samuel Johnson's Dictionary, he derived cricket from "cryce, Saxon, a stick". In Old French, the word "criquet" seems to have meant a kind of club or stick. Given the strong medieval trade connections between south-east England and the County of Flanders when the latter belonged to the Duchy of Burgundy, the name may have been derived from the Middle Dutch (in use in Flanders at the time) "krick"(-e), meaning a stick (crook). Another possible source is the Middle Dutch word "krickstoel", meaning a long low stool used for kneeling in church and which resembled the long low wicket with two stumps used in early cricket. According to Heiner Gillmeister, a European language expert of Bonn University, "cricket" derives from the Middle Dutch phrase for hockey, met de (krik ket)sen (i.e., "with the stick chase"). Gillmeister has suggested that not only the name but also the sport itself may be of Flemish origin.

- **Growth of amateur and professional cricket in England**

Evolution of the cricket bat. The original "hockey stick" (left) evolved into the straight bat from c. 1760 when pitched delivery bowling began.

Although the main object of the game has always been to score the most runs, the early form of cricket differed from the modern game in certain key technical aspects; the North American variant of cricket known as wicket retained many of these aspects. The ball was bowled underarm by the bowler and along the ground towards a batter armed with a bat that in shape resembled a hockey stick; the batter defended a low, two-stump wicket; and runs were called notches because the scorers recorded them by notching tally sticks.

In 1611, the year Cotgrave's dictionary was published, ecclesiastical court records at Sidlesham in Sussex state that two parishioners, Bartholomew Wyatt and Richard Latter, failed to attend church on Easter Sunday because they were playing cricket. They were fined 12d each and ordered to do penance.This is the earliest mention of adult participation in cricket and it was around the same time that the earliest known organised inter-parish or village match was played – at Chevening, Kent. In 1624, a player called Jasper Vinall died after he was accidentally struck on the head during a match between two parish teams in Sussex.

Cricket remained a low-key local pursuit for much of the 17th century. It is known, through numerous references found in the records of ecclesiastical court cases, to have been proscribed at times by the Puritans before and during the Commonwealth. The problem was nearly always the issue of Sunday play as the Puritans considered cricket to be "profane" if played on the Sabbath, especially if large crowds or gambling were involved.

According to the social historian Derek Birley, there was a "great upsurge of sport after the Restoration" in 1660. Gambling on sport became a problem significant enough for Parliament to pass the 1664 Gambling Act, limiting stakes to £100 which was, in any case, a colossal sum exceeding the annual income of 99% of the population. Along with prizefighting, horse racing and blood sports, cricket was perceived to be a gambling sport.Rich patrons made matches for high stakes, forming teams in which they engaged the first professional players.By the end of the century, cricket had developed into a major sport that was spreading throughout England and was already being taken abroad by English mariners and colonisers – the earliest reference to cricket overseas is dated 1676. A 1697 newspaper report survives of "a great cricket match" played in Sussex "for fifty guineas apiece" – this is the earliest known contest that is generally considered a First Class match.

- The patrons, and other players from the social class known as the "gentry", began to classify themselves as "amateurs" to establish a clear distinction from the professionals, who were invariably members of the working class, even to the point of having separate changing and dining facilities. The gentry, including such high-ranking nobles as the Dukes of Richmond, exerted their honour code of noblesse oblige to claim rights of leadership in any sporting contests they took part in, especially as it was necessary for them to play alongside their "social inferiors" if they were to win their bets. In time, a perception took hold that the typical amateur who played in first-class cricket, until 1962 when amateurism was abolished, was someone with a public school education who had then gone to one of Cambridge or Oxford University – society insisted that such people were "officers and gentlemen" whose destiny was to provide leadership. In a purely financial sense, the cricketing amateur would theoretically claim expenses for playing while his professional counterpart played under contract and was paid a wage or match fee;

in practice, many amateurs claimed more than actual expenditure and the derisive term "shamateur" was coined to describe the practice.

· **The Young Cricketer, 1768**

The game underwent major development in the 18th century to become England's national sport.Its success was underwritten by the twin necessities of patronage and betting. Cricket was prominent in London as early as 1707 and, in the middle years of the century, large crowds flocked to matches on the Artillery Ground in Finsbury. The single wicket form of the sport attracted huge crowds and wagers to match, its popularity peaking in the 1748 season. Bowling underwent an evolution around 1760 when bowlers began to pitch the ball instead of rolling or skimming it towards the batter. This caused a revolution in bat design because, to deal with the bouncing ball, it was necessary to introduce the modern straight bat in place of the old "hockey stick" shape.

The Hambledon Club was founded in the 1760s and, for the next twenty years until the formation of Marylebone Cricket Club (MCC) and the opening of Lord's Old Ground in 1787, Hambledon was both the game's greatest club and its focal point. MCC quickly became the sport's premier club and the custodian of the Laws of Cricket. New Laws introduced in the latter part of the 18th century included the three stump wicket and leg before wicket (lbw).

The 19th century saw underarm bowling superseded by first roundarm and then overarm bowling. Both developments were controversial.Organisation of the game at county level led to the creation of the county clubs, starting with Sussex in 1839. In December 1889, the eight leading county clubs formed the official County Championship, which began in 1890.

The most famous player of the 19th century was W. G. Grace, who started his long and influential career in 1865. It was especially during the career of Grace that the distinction between amateurs and professionals became blurred by the existence of players like him who were nominally amateur but, in terms of their financial gain, de facto professional. Grace himself was said to have been paid more money for playing cricket than any professional.

The last two decades before the First World War have been called the "Golden Age of cricket". It is a nostalgic name prompted by the collective sense of loss resulting from the war, but the period did produce some great players and memorable matches, especially as organised competition at county and Test level developed.

• Cricket becomes an international sport

In 1844, the first-ever international match took place between the United States and Canada. In 1859, a team of English players went to North America on the first overseas tour. Meanwhile, the British Empire had been instrumental in spreading the game overseas and by the middle of the 19th century it had become well established in Australia, the Caribbean, India, Pakistan, New Zealand, North America and South Africa.

In 1862, an English team made the first tour of Australia. The first Australian team to travel overseas consisted of Aboriginal stockmen who toured England in 1868. The first One Day International match was played on 5 January 1971 between Australia and England at the Melbourne Cricket Ground.

In 1876–77, an England team took part in what was retrospectively recognised as the first-ever Test match at the Melbourne Cricket Ground against Australia. The rivalry between England and Australia gave birth to The Ashes in 1882, and this has remained Test cricket's most famous contest. Test cricket began to expand in 1888–89 when South Africa played England.

World cricket in the 20th century

The inter-war years were dominated by Australia's Don Bradman, statistically the greatest Test batter of all time. Test cricket continued to expand during the 20th century with the addition of the West Indies (1928), New Zealand (1930) and India (1932) before the Second World War and then Pakistan (1952), Sri Lanka (1982), Zimbabwe (1992), Bangladesh (2000), Ireland and Afghanistan (both 2018) in the post-war period. South Africa was banned from international cricket from 1970 to 1992 as part of the apartheid boycott.

The rise of limited overs cricket

Cricket entered a new era in 1963 when English counties introduced the limited overs variant. As it was sure to produce a result, limited overs cricket was lucrative and the number of matches increased. The first Limited Overs International was played in 1971 and the governing International Cricket Council (ICC), seeing its potential, staged the first limited overs Cricket World Cup in 1975. In the 21st century, a new limited overs form, Twenty20, made an immediate impact. On 22 June 2017, Afghanistan and Ireland became the 11th and 12th ICC full members, enabling them to play Test cricket.

- **A typical cricket field.**

In cricket, the rules of the game are specified in a code called The Laws of Cricket (hereinafter called "the Laws") which has a global remit. There are 42 Laws (always written with a capital "L"). The earliest known version of the code was drafted in 1744 and, since 1788, it has been owned and maintained by its custodian, the Marylebone Cricket Club (MCC) in London.

- **Playing area**

Cricket is a bat-and-ball game played on a cricket field between two teams of eleven players each. The field is usually circular or oval in shape and the edge of the playing area is marked by a boundary, which may be a fence, part of the stands, a rope, a painted line or a combination of these; the boundary must if possible be marked along its entire length.

In the approximate centre of the field is a rectangular pitch (see image, below) on which a wooden target called a wicket is sited at each end; the wickets are placed 22 yards (20 m) apart. The pitch is a flat surface 10 feet (3.0 m) wide, with very short grass that tends to be worn away as the game progresses (cricket can also be played on artificial surfaces, notably matting). Each wicket is made of three wooden stumps topped by two bails.

- **Cricket pitch and creases**

As illustrated above, the pitch is marked at each end with four white painted lines: a bowling crease, a popping crease and two return creases. The three stumps are aligned centrally on the bowling crease, which is eight feet eight inches long. The popping crease is drawn four feet in front of the bowling crease and parallel to it; although it is drawn as a twelve-foot line (six feet either side of the wicket), it is, in fact, unlimited in length. The return creases are drawn at right angles to the popping crease so that they intersect the ends of the bowling crease; each return crease is drawn as an eight-foot line, so that it extends four feet behind the bowling crease, but is also, in fact, unlimited in length.

Before a match begins, the team captains (who are also players) toss a coin to decide which team will bat first and so take the first innings. Innings is the term used for each phase of play in the match.In each innings, one team bats, attempting to score runs, while the other team bowls and fields the ball, attempting to restrict the scoring and dismiss the batters. When the first innings ends, the teams change roles; there can be two to four innings depending upon the type of match. A match with four scheduled innings is played over three to five days; a match with two scheduled innings is usually completed in a single day. During an innings, all eleven members of the fielding team take the field, but usually only two members of the batting team are on the field at any given time. The exception to this is if a batter has any type of illness or injury restricting his or her ability to run, in this case the batter is allowed a runner who can run between the wickets when the batter hits a scoring run or runs,though this does not apply in international cricket. The order of batters is usually announced just before the match, but it can be varied.

The main objective of each team is to score more runs than their opponents but, in some forms of cricket, it is also necessary to dismiss all of the opposition batters in their final innings in order to win the match, which would otherwise be drawn. If the team batting last is all out having scored fewer runs than their opponents, they are said to have "lost by n runs" (where n is the difference between the aggregate number of runs scored by the teams). If the team that bats last scores enough runs to win, it is said to have "won by n wickets", where n is the number of wickets left to fall. For example, a team that passes its opponents' total having lost six wickets (i.e., six of their batters have been dismissed) have won the match "by four wickets".

In a two-innings-a-side match, one team's combined first and second innings total may be less than the other side's first innings total. The team with the greater score is then said to have "won by an innings and n runs", and does not need to bat again: n is the difference between the two teams' aggregate scores. If the team batting last is all out, and both sides have scored the same number of runs, then the match is a tie; this result is quite rare in matches of two innings a side with only 62 happening in first-class matches from the earliest known instance in 1741 until January 2017. In the traditional form of the game, if the time allotted for the match expires before either side can win, then the game is declared a draw.

If the match has only a single innings per side, then a maximum number of overs applies to each innings. Such a match is called a "limited overs" or "one-day" match, and the side scoring more runs wins regardless of the number of wickets lost, so that a draw cannot occur. In some cases, ties are broken by having each team bat for a one-over innings known as a Super Over; subsequent Super Overs may be played if the first Super Over ends in a tie. If this kind of match is temporarily interrupted by bad weather, then a complex mathematical formula, known as the Duckworth–Lewis–Stern method after its developers, is often used to recalculate a new target score. A one-day match can also be declared a "no-result" if fewer than a previously agreed number of overs have been bowled by either team, in circumstances that make normal resumption of play impossible; for example, wet weather.

In all forms of cricket, the umpires can abandon the match if bad light or rain makes it impossible to continue. There have been instances of entire matches, even Test matches scheduled to be played over five days, being lost to bad weather without a ball being bowled: for example, the third Test of the 1970/71 series in Australia.

· **Innings**

The innings (ending with 's' in both singular and plural form) is the term used for each phase of play during a match. Depending on the type of match being played, each team has either one or two innings. Sometimes all eleven members of the batting side take a turn to bat but, for various reasons, an innings can end before they have all done so. The innings terminates if the batting team is "all out", a term defined by the Laws: "at the fall of a wicket or the retirement of a batter, further balls remain to be bowled but no further batter is available to come in". In this situation, one of the batters has not been dismissed and is termed not out; this is because he has no partners left and there must always be two active batters while the innings is in progress.

- **An innings may end early while there are still two not out batters**

the batting team's captain may declare the innings closed even though some of his players have not had a turn to bat: this is a tactical decision by the captain, usually because he believes his team have scored sufficient runs and need time to dismiss the opposition in their innings

the set number of overs (i.e., in a limited overs match) have been bowled

the match has ended prematurely due to bad weather or running out of time

in the final innings of the match, the batting side has reached its target and won the game.

- **Overs**

The Laws state that, throughout an innings, "the ball shall be bowled from each end alternately in overs of 6 balls". The name "over" came about because the umpire calls "Over!" when six balls have been bowled. At this point, another bowler is deployed at the other end, and the fielding side changes ends while the batters do not. A bowler cannot bowl two successive overs, although a bowler can (and usually does) bowl alternate overs, from the same end, for several overs which are termed a "spell". The batters do not change ends at the end of the over, and so the one who was non-striker is now the striker and vice versa. The umpires also change positions so that the one who was at "square leg" now stands behind the wicket at the non-striker's end and vice versa.

- **Clothing and equipment**

English cricketer W. G. Grace "taking guard" in 1883. His pads and bat are very similar to those used today. The gloves have evolved somewhat. Many modern players use more defensive equipment than were available to Grace, most notably helmets and arm guards.

The wicket-keeper (a specialised fielder behind the batter) and the batters wear protective gear because of the hardness of the ball, which can be delivered at speeds of more than 145 kilometres per hour (90 mph) and presents a major health and safety concern. Protective clothing includes pads (designed to protect the knees and shins), batting gloves or wicket-keeper's gloves for the hands, a safety helmet for the head and a box for male players inside the trousers (to protect the crotch area). Some batters wear additional padding inside their shirts and trousers such as thigh pads, arm pads, rib protectors and shoulder pads. The only fielders allowed to wear protective gear are those in positions very close to the batter (i.e., if they are alongside or in front of him), but they cannot wear gloves or external leg guards.

Subject to certain variations, on-field clothing generally includes a collared shirt with short or long sleeves; long trousers; woolen pullover (if needed); cricket cap (for fielding) or a safety helmet; and spiked shoes or boots to increase traction. The kit is traditionally all white and this remains the case in Test and first-class cricket but, in limited overs cricket, team colours are worn instead.

- **Bat and ball**

Two types of cricket ball, both of the same size:
i) A used white ball. White balls are mainly used in limited overs cricket, especially in matches played at night,

under floodlights (left).

ii) A used red ball. Red balls are used in Test cricket, first-class cricket and some other forms of cricket (right).

The essence of the sport is that a bowler delivers (i.e., bowls) the ball from his or her end of the pitch towards the batter who, armed with a bat, is "on strike" at the other end (see next sub-section: Basic gameplay).

The bat is made of wood, usually Salix alba (white willow), and has the shape of a blade topped by a cylindrical handle. The blade must not be more than 4.25 inches (10.8 cm) wide and the total length of the bat not more than 38 inches (97 cm). There is no standard for the weight, which is usually between 2 lb 7 oz and 3 lb (1.1 and 1.4 kg).

The ball is a hard leather-seamed spheroid, with a circumference of 9 inches (23 cm). The ball has a "seam": six rows of stitches attaching the leather shell of the ball to the string and cork interior. The seam on a new ball is prominent and helps the bowler propel it in a less predictable manner. During matches, the quality of the ball deteriorates to a point where it is no longer usable; during the course of this deterioration, its behaviour in flight will change and can influence the outcome of the match. Players will, therefore, attempt to modify the ball's behaviour by modifying its physical properties. Polishing the ball and wetting it with sweat or saliva is legal, even when the polishing is deliberately done on one side only to increase the ball's swing through the air, but the acts of rubbing other substances into the ball, scratching the surface or picking at the seam are illegal ball tampering.

- **Player roles**

Basic gameplay: bowler to batter

During normal play, thirteen players and two umpires are on the field. Two of the players are batters and the rest are all eleven members of the fielding team. The other nine players in the batting team are off the field in the pavilion. The image with overlay below shows what is happening when a ball is being bowled and which of the personnel are on or close to the pitch.

- **Return crease**

In the photo, the two batters (3 & 8; wearing yellow) have taken position at each end of the pitch (6). Three members of the fielding team (4, 10 & 11; wearing dark blue) are in shot. One of the two umpires (1; wearing white hat) is stationed behind the wicket (2) at the bowler's (4) end of the pitch. The bowler (4) is bowling the ball (5) from his end of the pitch to the batter at the other end who is called the "striker". The other batter (3) at the bowling end is called the "non-striker". The wicket-keeper (10), who is a specialist, is positioned behind the striker's wicket (9) and behind him stands one of the fielders in a position called "first slip" (11). While the bowler and the first slip are wearing conventional kit only, the two batters and the wicket-keeper are wearing protective gear including safety helmets, padded gloves and leg guards (pads).

While the umpire (1) in shot stands at the bowler's end of the pitch, his colleague stands in the outfield, usually in or near the fielding position called "square leg", so that he is in line with the popping crease (7) at the striker's end of the pitch. The bowling crease (not numbered) is the one on which the wicket is located between the return creases (12). The bowler (4) intends to hit the wicket (9) with the ball (5) or, at least, to prevent the striker (8) from scoring runs. The striker (8) intends, by using his bat, to defend his wicket and, if possible, to hit the ball away from the pitch in order to score runs.

Some players are skilled in both batting and bowling, or as either or these as well as wicket-keeping, so are termed all-rounders. Bowlers are classified according to their style, generally as fast bowlers, seam bowlers or spinners. Batters are classified according to whether they are right-handed or left-handed.

· Fielding

Of the eleven fielders, three are in shot in the image above. The other eight are elsewhere on the field, their positions determined on a tactical basis by the captain or the bowler. Fielders often change position between deliveries, again as directed by the captain or bowler.

If a fielder is injured or becomes ill during a match, a substitute is allowed to field instead of him, but the substitute cannot bowl or act as a captain, except in the case of concussion substitutes in international cricket. The substitute leaves the field when the injured player is fit to return. The Laws of Cricket were updated in 2017 to allow substitutes to act as wicket-keepers.

· Bowling and dismissal

Glenn McGrath of Australia holds the world record for most wickets in the Cricket World Cup.

Most bowlers are considered specialists in that they are selected for the team because of their skill as a bowler, although some are all-rounders and even specialist batters bowl occasionally. The specialists bowl several times during an innings but may not bowl two overs consecutively. If the captain wants a bowler to "change ends", another bowler must temporarily fill in so that the change is not immediate.

A bowler reaches his delivery stride by means of a "run-up" and an over is deemed to have begun when the bowler starts his run-up for the first delivery of that over, the ball then being "in play".

Fast bowlers, needing momentum, take a lengthy run up while bowlers with a slow delivery take no more than a couple of steps before bowling. The fastest bowlers can deliver the ball at a speed of over 145 kilometres per hour (90 mph) and they sometimes rely on sheer speed to try to defeat the batter, who is forced to react very quickly.

Other fast bowlers rely on a mixture of speed and guile by making the ball seam or swing (i.e. curve) in flight. This type of delivery can deceive a batter into miscuing his shot, for example, so that the ball just touches the edge of the bat and can then be "caught behind" by the wicket-keeper or a slip fielder. At the other end of the bowling scale is the spin bowler who bowls at a relatively slow pace and relies entirely on guile to deceive the batter. A spinner will often "buy his wicket" by "tossing one up" (in a slower, steeper parabolic path) to lure the batter into making a poor shot. The batter has to be very wary of such deliveries as they are often "flighted" or spun so that the ball will not behave quite as he expects and he could be "trapped" into getting himself out. In between the pacemen and the spinners are the medium paced seamers who rely on persistent accuracy to try to contain the rate of scoring and wear down the batter's concentration.

There are nine ways in which a batter can be dismissed: five relatively common and four extremely rare. The common forms of dismissal are bowled, caught, leg before wicket (lbw), run out and stumped. Rare methods are hit wicket,hit the ball twice, obstructing the field and timed out. The Laws state that the fielding team, usually the bowler in practice, must appeal for a dismissal before the umpire can give his decision. If the batter is out, the umpire raises a forefinger and says "Out!"; otherwise, he will shake his head and say "Not out".There is, effectively, a tenth method of dismissal, retired out, which is not an on-field dismissal as such but rather a retrospective one for which no fielder is credited.

- **Batting, runs and extras**

The directions in which a right-handed batter, facing down the page, intends to send the ball when playing various cricketing shots. The diagram for a left-handed batter is a mirror image of this one.

Batters take turns to bat via a batting order which is decided beforehand by the team captain and presented to the umpires, though the order remains flexible when the captain officially nominates the team. Substitute batters are generally not allowed, except in the case of concussion substitutes in international cricket.

In order to begin batting the batter first adopts a batting stance. Standardly, this involves adopting a slight crouch with the feet pointing across the front of the wicket, looking in the direction of the bowler, and holding the bat so it passes over the feet and so its tip can rest on the ground near to the toes of the back foot.

A skilled batter can use a wide array of "shots" or "strokes" in both defensive and attacking mode. The idea is to hit the ball to the best effect with the flat surface of the bat's blade. If the ball touches the side of the bat it is called an "edge". The batter does not have to play a shot and can allow the ball to go through to the wicketkeeper. Equally, he does not have to attempt a run when he hits the ball with his bat. Batters do not always seek to hit the ball as hard as possible, and a good player can score runs just by making a deft stroke with a turn of the wrists or by simply "blocking" the ball but directing it away from fielders so that he has time to take a run. A wide variety of shots are played, the batter's repertoire including strokes named according to the style of swing and the direction aimed: e.g., "cut", "drive", "hook", "pull".

The batter on strike (i.e. the "striker") must prevent the ball hitting the wicket, and try to score runs by hitting the ball with his bat so that he and his partner have time to run from one end of the pitch to the other before the fielding side can return the ball. To register a run, both runners must touch the ground behind the popping crease with either their bats or their bodies (the batters carry their bats as they run). Each completed run increments the score of both the team and the striker.

- **Sachin Tendulkar is the only player to have scored one hundred international centuries**

The decision to attempt a run is ideally made by the batter who has the better view of the ball's progress, and this is communicated by calling: usually "yes", "no" or "wait". More than one run can be scored from a single hit: hits worth one to three runs are common, but the size of the field is such that it is usually difficult to run four or more. To compensate for this, hits that reach the boundary of the field are automatically awarded four runs if the ball touches the ground en route to the boundary or six runs if the ball clears the boundary without touching the ground within the boundary. In these cases the batters do not need to run. Hits for five are unusual and generally rely on the help of "overthrows" by a fielder returning the ball. If an odd number of runs is scored by the striker, the two batters have changed ends, and the one who was non-striker is now the striker. Only the striker can score individual runs, but all runs are added to the team's total.

Additional runs can be gained by the batting team as extras (called "sundries" in Australia) due to errors made by the fielding side. This is achieved in four ways: no-ball, a penalty of one extra conceded by the bowler if he breaks the rules; wide, a penalty of one extra conceded by the bowler if he bowls so that the ball is out of the batter's reach bye, an extra awarded if the batter misses the ball and it goes past the wicket-keeper and gives the batters time to run in the conventional way leg bye, as for a bye except that the ball has hit the batter's body, though not his bat. If the bowler has conceded a no-ball or a wide, his team incurs an additional penalty because that ball (i.e., delivery) has to be bowled again and hence the batting side has the opportunity to score more runs from this extra ball.

- **Specialist roles**

Captain (cricket) and Wicket-keeper

The captain is often the most experienced player in the team, certainly the most tactically astute, and can possess any of the main skillsets as a batter, a bowler or a wicket-keeper. Within the Laws, the captain has certain responsibilities in terms of nominating his players to the umpires before the match and ensuring that his players conduct themselves "within the spirit and traditions of the game as well as within the Laws".

The wicket-keeper (sometimes called simply the "keeper") is a specialist fielder subject to various rules within the Laws about his equipment and demeanour. He is the only member of the fielding side who can effect a stumping and is the only one permitted to wear gloves and external leg guards. Depending on their primary skills, the other ten players in the team tend to be classified as specialist batters or specialist bowlers. Generally, a team will include five or six specialist batters and four or five specialist bowlers, plus the wicket-keeper.

· Umpires and scorers

The game on the field is regulated by the two umpires, one of whom stands behind the wicket at the bowler's end, the other in a position called "square leg" which is about 15–20 metres away from the batter on strike and in line with the popping crease on which he is taking guard. The umpires have several responsibilities including adjudication on whether a ball has been correctly bowled (i.e., not a no-ball or a wide); when a run is scored; whether a batter is out (the fielding side must first appeal to the umpire, usually with the phrase "How's that?" or "Owzat?"); when intervals start and end; and the suitability of the pitch, field and weather for playing the game. The umpires are authorised to interrupt or even abandon a match due to circumstances likely to endanger the players, such as a damp pitch or deterioration of the light.

Off the field in televised matches, there is usually a third umpire who can make decisions on certain incidents with the aid of video evidence. The third umpire is mandatory under the playing conditions for Test and Limited Overs

International matches played between two ICC full member countries. These matches also have a match referee whose job is to ensure that play is within the Laws and the spirit of the game.

The match details, including runs and dismissals, are recorded by two official scorers, one representing each team. The scorers are directed by the hand signals of an umpire . For example, the umpire raises a forefinger to signal that the batter is out (has been dismissed); he raises both arms above his head if the batter has hit the ball for six runs. The scorers are required by the Laws to record all runs scored, wickets taken and overs bowled; in practice, they also note significant amounts of additional data relating to the game.

A match's statistics are summarised on a scorecard. Prior to the popularisation of scorecards, most scoring was done by men sitting on vantage points cuttings notches on tally sticks and runs were originally called notches.According to Rowland Bowen, the earliest known scorecard templates were introduced in 1776 by T. Pratt of Sevenoaks and soon came into general use.It is believed that scorecards were printed and sold at Lord's for the first time in 1846.

FOUR

HISTORY OF CRICKET

- **History of cricket**

The sport of cricket has a known history beginning in the late 16th century. Having originated in south-east England, it became an established sport in the country in the 18th century and developed globally in the 19th and 20th centuries. International matches have been played since the 19th-century and formal Test cricket matches are considered to date from 1877. Cricket is the world's second most popular spectator sport after association football (soccer).

Internationally, cricket is governed by the International Cricket Council (ICC) which has over one hundred countries and territories in membership although only twelve currently play Test cricket.

- **Origin**

Cricket was probably created during Saxon or Norman times by children living in the Weald, an area of dense woodlands and clearings in south-east England that lies across Kent and Sussex. The first definite written reference is from the end of the 16th-century.

There have been several speculations about the game's origins, including some that it was created in France or Flanders. The earliest of these speculative references is from 1300 and concerns the future King Edward II playing at "creag and other games" in both Westminster and Newenden. It has been suggested that "creag" was an Old English word for cricket, but expert opinion is that it was an early spelling of "craic", meaning "fun and games in general".

It is generally believed that cricket survived as a children's game for many generations before it was increasingly taken up by adults around the beginning of the 17th century. Possibly cricket was derived from bowls, assuming bowls is the older sport, by the intervention of a batsman trying to stop the ball from reaching its target by hitting it away. Playing on sheep-grazed land or in clearings, the original implements may have been a matted lump of sheep's wool (or even a stone or a small lump of wood) as the ball; a stick or a crook or another farm tool as the bat; and a stool or a tree stump or a gate (e.g., a wicket gate) as the wicket.

- **First definite reference**

John Derrick was a pupil at the Royal Grammar School, then the Free School, in Guildford when he and his friends played creckett circa 1550.

In 1597 (Old Style – 1598 New Style) a court case in England concerning an ownership dispute over a plot of common land in Guildford, Surrey, mentions the game of creckett. A 59-year-old coroner, John Derrick, testified that he and his school friends had played creckett on the site fifty years earlier when they attended the Free School. Derrick's account proves beyond reasonable doubt that the game was being played in Surrey circa 1550, and is the earliest universally accepted reference to the game.

The first reference to cricket being played as an adult sport was in 1611, when two men in Sussex were prosecuted for playing cricket on Sunday instead of going to church. In the same year, a dictionary defined cricket as a boys' game, and this suggests that adult participation was a recent development.

· **Derivation of the name of "cricket"**

A number of words are thought to be possible sources for the term "cricket". In the earliest definite reference, it was spelled creckett. The name may have been derived from the Middle Dutch krick(-e), meaning a stick; or the Old English cricc or cryce meaning a crutch or staff, or the French word criquet meaning a wooden post. The Middle Dutch word krickstoel means a long low stool used for kneeling in church; this resembled the long low wicket with two stumps used in early cricket. According to Heiner Gillmeister, a European language expert of the University of Bonn, "cricket" derives from the Middle Dutch phrase for hockey, met de (krik ket)sen (i.e., "with the stick chase").

It is more likely that the terminology of cricket was based on words in use in south-east England at the time and, given trade connections with the County of Flanders, especially in the 15th century when it belonged to the Duchy of Burgundy, many Middle Dutch words found their way into southern English dialects.

· The Commonwealth

After the Civil War ended in 1648, the new Puritan government clamped down on "unlawful assemblies", in particular the more raucous sports such as football. Their laws also demanded a stricter observance of the Sabbath than there had been previously. As the Sabbath was the only free time available to the lower classes, cricket's popularity may have waned during the Commonwealth. However, it did flourish in public fee-paying schools such as Winchester and St Paul's. There is no actual evidence that Oliver Cromwell's regime banned cricket specifically and there are references to it during the interregnum that suggest it was acceptable to the authorities provided that it did not cause any "breach of the Sabbath". It is believed that the nobility in general adopted cricket at this time through involvement in village games.

· Gambling and press coverage

Cricket thrived after the Restoration in 1660 and is believed to have first attracted gamblers making large bets at this time. It is possible, as believed by some historians, that top-class matches began. In 1664, the "Cavalier" Parliament passed the Gaming Act 1664 which limited stakes to £100, although that was still a fortune at the time, equivalent to about £16,000 in present-day terms. Cricket had become a significant gambling sport by the end of the 17th century, as evidenced in 1697 by a newspaper report of a "great match" played in Sussex which was 11-a-side and played for high stakes of 50 guineas a side.

With freedom of the press having been granted in 1696, cricket for the first time could be reported in the newspapers. But it was a long time before the newspaper industry adapted sufficiently to provide frequent, let alone comprehensive, coverage of the game. During the first half of the 18th century, press reports tended to focus on the betting rather than on the play.

- **18th-century cricket**

Gambling introduced the first patrons because some of the gamblers decided to strengthen their bets by forming their own teams and it is believed the first "county teams" were formed in the aftermath of the Restoration in 1660, especially as members of the nobility were employing "local experts" from village cricket as the earliest professionals. The first known game in which the teams use county names is in 1709 but there can be little doubt that these sort of fixtures were being arranged long before that. The match in 1697 was probably Sussex versus another county.

The most notable of the early patrons were a group of aristocrats and businessmen who were active from about 1725, which is the time that press coverage became more regular, perhaps as a result of the patrons' influence. These men included the 2nd Duke of Richmond, Sir William Gage, Alan Brodrick and Edwin Stead. For the first time, the press mentions individual players like Thomas Waymark.

- **Cricket expands beyond England**

Cricket was introduced to North America via the English colonies in the 17th century, probably before it had even reached the north of England. In the 18th century it arrived in other parts of the globe. It was introduced to the West Indies by colonists and to India by East India Company mariners in the first half of the century. It arrived in Australia almost as soon as colonisation began in 1788. New Zealand and South Africa followed in the early years of the 19th century.

Cricket never caught on in Canada, despite efforts by the upper class to promote the game as a way of identifying with the "mother country". Canada, unlike Australia and the West Indies, witnessed a continual decline in the popularity of the game during 1860 to 1960. Linked in the public consciousness to an upper-class sport, the game never became popular with the general public. In the summer season it had to compete with baseball. During the First World War, Canadian units stationed in France played baseball instead of cricket.

- **Development Laws of Cricket**

It's not clear when the basic rules of cricket such as bat and ball, the wicket, pitch dimensions, overs, how out, etc. were originally formulated. In 1728, the Duke of Richmond and Alan Brodick drew up Articles of Agreement to determine the code of practice in a particular game and this became a common feature, especially around payment of stake money and distributing the winnings given the importance of gambling.

In 1744, the Laws of Cricket were codified for the first time and then amended in 1774, when innovations such as lbw, middle stump and maximum bat width were added.

These laws stated that "the principals shall choose from amongst the gentlemen present two umpires who shall absolutely decide all disputes". The codes were drawn up by the so-called "Star and Garter Club" whose members ultimately founded the Marylebone Cricket Club at Lord's in 1787. The MCC immediately became the custodian of the Laws and has made periodic revisions and recodifications subsequently.

- **Continued growth in England**

The game continued to spread throughout England, and, in 1751, Yorkshire is first mentioned as a venue. The original form of bowling (i.e., rolling the ball along the ground as in bowls) was superseded sometime after 1760 when bowlers began to pitch the ball and study variations in line, length and pace. Scorecards began to be kept on a regular basis from 1772; since then, an increasingly clear picture has emerged of the sport's development.

- **An artwork depicting the history of the cricket bat**

The first famous clubs were London and Dartford in the early 18th century. London played its matches on the Artillery Ground, which still exists. Others followed, particularly Slindon in Sussex, which was backed by the Duke of Richmond and featured the star player Richard Newland. There were other prominent clubs at Maidenhead, Hornchurch, Maidstone, Sevenoaks, Bromley, Addington, Hadlow and Chertsey.

But far and away the most famous of the early clubs was Hambledon in Hampshire. It started as a parish organisation that first achieved prominence in 1756. The club itself was founded in the 1760s and was well patronised to the extent that it was the focal point of the game for about thirty years until the formation of MCC and the opening of Lord's Cricket Ground in 1787. Hambledon produced several outstanding players including the master batsman John Small and the first great fast bowler Thomas Brett. Their most notable opponent was the Chertsey and Surrey bowler Edward "Lumpy" Stevens, who is believed to have been the main proponent of the flighted delivery.

It was in answer to the flighted, or pitched, delivery that the straight bat was introduced. The old "hockey stick"–style of bat was only really effective against the ball being trundled or skimmed along the ground. First-class cricket began, retrospectively, in 1772. A Game of Cricket at The Royal Academy Club in Marylebone Fields, now Regent's Park, depiction by unknown artist, c. 1790–1799

- **History of cricket (1772–1815) and History of English cricket (1816–1863)**

The game also underwent a fundamental change of organisation with the formation for the first time of county clubs. All the modern county clubs, starting with Sussex in 1839, were founded during the 19th century. No sooner had the first county clubs established themselves than they faced what amounted to "player action" as William Clarke created the travelling All-England Eleven in 1846. Though a commercial venture, this team did much to popularise the game in districts which had never previously been visited by high-class cricketers. Other similar teams were created and this vogue lasted for about thirty years. But the counties and MCC prevailed.

- **A cricket match at Darnall, Sheffield in the 1820s.**

The growth of cricket in the mid and late 19th century was assisted by the development of the railway network. For the first time, teams from a long distance apart could play one other without a prohibitively time-consuming journey. Spectators could travel longer distances to matches, increasing the size of crowds. Army units around the Empire had time on their hands, and encouraged the locals so they could have some entertaining competition. Most of the Empire embraced cricket, with the exception of Canada.

In 1864, another bowling revolution resulted in the legalisation of overarm and in the same year. W. G. Grace began his long and influential career at this time, his feats doing much to increase cricket's popularity. He introduced technical innovations which revolutionised the game, particularly in batting.

- **International cricket begins**

The first ever international cricket game was between the US and Canada in 1844. The match was played at the grounds of the St George's Cricket Club in New York.

- **The English team 1859 on their way to the US**

In 1859, a team of leading English professionals set off to North America on the first-ever overseas tour and, in 1862, the first English team toured Australia. Between May and October 1868, a team of Aboriginal Australians toured England in what was the first Australian cricket team to travel overseas.

- **The first Australian touring team (1878) pictured at Niagara Falls**

In 1877, an England touring team in Australia played two matches against full Australian XIs that are now regarded as the inaugural Test matches. The following year, the Australians toured England for the first time and the success of this tour ensured a popular demand for similar ventures in future. No Tests were played in 1878 but more soon followed and, at The Oval in 1882, the Australian victory in a tense finish gave rise to The Ashes.South Africa became the third Test nation in 1889.

- **National championships**

A significant development in domestic cricket occurred in 1890 when the official County Championship was constituted in England. Soon afterwards, in May 1894, the sport's first-class standard was officially defined. This organisational initiative has been repeated in other countries. Australia established the Sheffield Shield in 1892–93. Other national competitions to be established were the Currie Cup in South Africa, the Plunket Shield in New Zealand and the Ranji Trophy in India. The ICC re-defined first-class status in 1947 as a global concept.

The period from 1890 to the outbreak of the First World War has become one of nostalgia, ostensibly because the teams played cricket according to "the spirit of the game", but more realistically because it was a peacetime period that was shattered by the First World War. The era has been called The Golden Age of cricket and it featured numerous great names such as Grace, Wilfred Rhodes, C. B. Fry, Ranjitsinhji and Victor Trumper.

· **Balls per over**

During most of the 19th-century standard overs were
made up of four deliveries. In 1889 five-ball overs were
introduced in first-class cricket, with a move to generally
use six-ball overs in 1900.

In the 20th-century, eight-ball overs were used at times
in a number of countries, primarily Australia, where eight-
balls were the standard over length between 1918/19 and
1978/79, South Africa and New Zealand. Since the 1979/80
Australian and New Zealand seasons, six balls per over have
been used worldwide, and the most recent version of the
Laws only permits six-ball overs.

· **Growth of international cricket**

Sid Barnes traps Lala Amarnath lbw in the first official
Test between Australia and India at the MCG in 1948

The Imperial Cricket Conference was founded in 1909
with England, Australia and South Africa as the founder
members. This aimed to regulate international cricket
between the three sides, considered the only three of equal
status at the time. West Indies were admitted as members
in 1928, allowing them to play Test cricket against the other
sides. New Zealand and India both became Test playing
nations before World War II and Pakistan joined soon
afterwards in 1952.

At the initial suggestion of Pakistan, the ICC was
expanded to include non-Test playing countries from 1965,
with Associate members being admitted. At the same time
the organisation changed its name to the International
Cricket Conference. The first limited-overs World Cups were
played during the 1970s and Sri Lanka became the first

Associate member to be raised to Test playing status in 1982.

The international game continued to grow with the introduction of Affiliate Member status in 1984, a level of membership designed for sides with less history of playing cricket. In 1989 the ICC renamed itself the International Cricket Council. Zimbabwe became Full Members in 1992 and Bangladesh in 2000 before Afghanistan and Ireland were both admitted as Test sides in 2018, bringing the number of full members of the ICC to 12.

- **International cricket in South Africa from 1971 to 1981**

The greatest crisis to hit international cricket was brought about by apartheid, the South African policy of racial segregation. The situation began to crystallise after 1961 when South Africa left the Commonwealth of Nations and so, under the rules of the day, its cricket board had to leave the International Cricket Conference (ICC). Cricket's opposition to apartheid intensified in 1968 with the cancellation of England's tour to South Africa by the South African authorities, due to the inclusion in the England team of Basil D'Oliveira, a Cape Coloured player. In 1970, the ICC members voted to suspend South Africa indefinitely from international cricket competition.

Starved of top-level competition for its best players, the South African Cricket Board began funding so-called "rebel tours", offering large sums of money for international players to form teams and tour South Africa. The ICC's response was to blacklist any rebel players who agreed to tour South Africa, banning them from officially sanctioned international cricket. As players were poorly remunerated during the 1970s, several accepted the offer to tour South Africa, particularly players getting towards the end of their careers for which a blacklisting would have little effect.

The rebel tours continued into the 1980s but then progress was made in South African politics and it became clear that apartheid was ending. South Africa, now a "Rainbow Nation" under Nelson Mandela, was welcomed back into international sport in 1991.

- ### World Series Cricket

The money problems of top cricketers were also the root cause of another cricketing crisis that arose in 1977 when the Australian media magnate Kerry Packer fell out with the Australian Cricket Board over TV rights. Taking advantage of the low remuneration paid to players, Packer retaliated by signing several of the best players in the world to a privately run cricket league outside the structure of international cricket. World Series Cricket hired some of the banned South African players and allowed them to show off their skills in an international arena against other world-class players. The schism lasted only until 1979 and the "rebel" players were allowed back into established international cricket, though many found that their national teams had moved on without them. Long-term results of World Series Cricket have included the introduction of significantly higher player salaries and innovations such as coloured kit and night games.

- ### Limited-overs cricket

In the 1960s, English county teams began playing a version of cricket with games of only one innings each and a maximum number of overs per innings. Starting in 1963 as a knockout competition only, limited-overs cricket grew in popularity and, in 1969, a national league was created which consequently caused a reduction in the number of matches in the County Championship. The status of limited overs matches is governed by the official List A categorisation. Although many "traditional" cricket fans objected to the shorter form of the game, limited-overs cricket did have the advantage of delivering a result to spectators within a single day; it did improve cricket's appeal to younger or busier people; and it did prove commercially successful.

The first limited-overs international match took place at Melbourne Cricket Ground in 1971 as a time-filler after a Test match had been abandoned because of heavy rain on the opening days. It was tried simply as an experiment and to give the players some exercise, but turned out to be immensely popular. limited-overs internationals (LOIs or ODIs—one-day internationals) have since grown to become a massively popular form of the game, especially for busy people who want to be able to see a whole match. The International Cricket Council reacted to this development by organising the first Cricket World Cup in England in 1975, with all the Test-playing nations taking part.

- **Analytic and graphic technology**

Limited-overs cricket increased television ratings for cricket coverage. Innovative techniques introduced in coverage of limited-over matches were soon adopted for Test coverage. The innovations included presentation of in-depth statistics and graphical analysis, placing miniature cameras in the stumps, multiple usage of cameras to provide shots from several locations around the ground, high-speed photography and computer graphics technology enabling television viewers to study the course of a delivery and help them understand an umpire's decision.

In 1992, the use of a third umpire to adjudicate run-out appeals with television replays was introduced in the Test series between South Africa and India. The third umpire's duties have subsequently expanded to include decisions on other aspects of play such as stumpings, catches and boundaries. From 2011, the third umpire was being called upon to moderate review of umpires' decisions, including lbw, with the aid of virtual-reality tracking technologies (e.g., Hawk-Eye and Hot Spot), though such measures still could not free some disputed decisions from heated controversy.

- **21st-century cricket**

In June 2001, the ICC introduced a "Test Championship Table" and, in October 2002, a "One-day International Championship Table". As indicated by ICC rankings, the various cricket formats have continued to be a major competitive sport in most former British Empire countries, notably the Indian subcontinent, and new participants including the Netherlands. In 2017, the number of countries with full ICC membership was increased to twelve by the addition of Afghanistan and Ireland.

The ICC expanded its development programme, aiming to produce more national teams capable of competing at the various formats. Development efforts are focused on African and Asian nations, and on the United States. In 2004, the ICC Intercontinental Cup brought first-class cricket to 12 nations, mostly for the first time. Cricket's newest innovation is Twenty20, essentially an evening entertainment. It has so far enjoyed enormous popularity and has attracted large attendances at matches as well as good TV audience ratings. The inaugural ICC Twenty20 World Cup tournament was held in 2007. The formation of Twenty20 leagues in India – the unofficial Indian Cricket League, which started in 2007, and the official Indian Premier League, starting in 2008 – raised much speculation in the cricketing press about their effect on the future of cricket.

* 9 7 9 8 8 8 9 2 3 2 4 3 8 *